Texts and Contexts

The idea of studying texts 'in context' has become a major new emphasis in contemporary literary studies. This book explores the idea of contexts and the way they affect texts, concentrating upon:

◎   the writer's context
◎   the reader's context
◎   the text's context
◎   the language context
◎   the meaning context

Through a series of units comprising texts, exercises and commentaries, Adrian Beard sets out a framework for studying texts and their contexts. He encourages students to think about the contexts in which they and other readers interpret a text, exploring the way in which texts mean different things to different people at different times.

This is the ideal starting point for anyone new to contextualised reading.

Adrian Beard teaches at Gosforth High School, Newcastle upon Tyne, and is Chief Examiner for AS/A level English Literature. He is a series editor for Intertext (Routledge) and his previous publications include *The Language of Sport* (Routledge: 1998) and *The Language of Politics* (Routledge: 1999).

A teachers' guide is available free to teachers of AS or A2 courses in the UK. Please call Routledge Customer Services on 01264 342 939, quoting ISBN 0–415–25718–2. The full text of the teachers' guide is available on the Routledge website at http://www.routledge.com/textbooks/textsandcontexts.html

Texts and Contexts

Introducing literature and language study

• Adrian Beard

London and New York

First published 2001
by Routledge
11 New Fetter Lane, London EC4P 4EE

Simultaneously published in the USA
and Canada
by Routledge
29 West 35th Street, New York,
NY 10001

*Routledge is an imprint of the
Taylor & Francis Group*

Typeset in Stone Sans / Stone Serif by
Bookcraft Ltd, Stroud, Gloucestershire

Printed and bound in Great Britain by
TJ International Ltd, Padstow, Cornwall

*British Library Cataloguing in Publication
Data*
A catalogue record for this book is available
from the British Library

*Library of Congress Cataloguing in
Publication Data*
Beard, Adrian, 1951–
    Texts and contexts: introducing
literature and language study / Adrian
Beard.
        p.   cm.
    Includes bibliographical references.
    1. English literature – History and
criticism – Outlines, syllabi, etc.
    2. English literature – History and
criticism – Problems, exercises, etc.
    3. Literature and history – Great Britain –
Outlines, syllabi, etc. 4. Literature and
history –Great Britain – Problems,
exercises, etc. 5. Historicism – Problems,
exercises, etc. I. Title.
    PR25 .B43 2001
    820.9–dc21   00–051833

ISBN 0–415–25350–0 (hbk)
ISBN 0–415–22987–1 (pbk)

contents

Acknowledgements   vii

1 Texts and contexts: a framework   1

2 Texts and contexts: whose dog are you?   9

Epigram   Alexander Pope   9

3 Texts and contexts: raising the *Titanic*   15

The Convergence of the Twain   Thomas Hardy   18
Every Man for Himself   Beryl Bainbridge   24
Some Unmentioned Morals   G.B. Shaw   27

4 Attitudes, values and assumptions   33

Nurofen advertisement   35
Sense and Sensibility   Jane Austen   38
Huckleberry Finn   Mark Twain   45
Robinson Crusoe   Daniel Defoe   50

5 Finding meanings in poetry   55

Mr Bleaney   Philip Larkin   56
The Patriot   Robert Browning   61
Sonnet 26 From the Portuguese   Elizabeth Barrett Browning   66

6 Making readings in drama   73

Macbeth   William Shakespeare   76
The Tempest   William Shakespeare   78
Hamlet   William Shakespeare   86
Much Ado About Nothing   William Shakespeare   90
She Stoops to Conquer   Oliver Goldsmith   95

7 Contexts and Shakespeare
(co-authored by Margaret Walker)   **101**

The Taming of the Shrew   William Shakespeare   110

8 Similarity and difference   **119**

Sonnet 18   William Shakespeare   122
Sonnet 130   William Shakespeare   124
Hekatompathia   Thomas Watson   126
Great Expectations   Charles Dickens   127
Jack Maggs   Peter Carey   131

9 Critical viewpoints   **149**

The Going   Thomas Hardy   150

Index of terms   163

acknowledgements

Thanks to students of Gosforth High School, Newcastle upon Tyne, for their help with trials of some of the material in this book. Thanks also to Margaret Walker for her contributions to the Shakespeare material and to Amanda Coultas for her helpful comments.

The author and publishers wish to thank the following for permission to reprint copyright material: Crookes Healthcare Ltd for the *Nurofen* advertisement; Beryl Bainbridge and Gerald Duckworth and Co. Ltd for the extract from Beryl Bainbridge's *Every Man for Himself*; Faber & Faber for *Mr Bleaney* by Philip Larkin; Peter Carey and Faber & Faber for the extract from *Jack Maggs*.

Routledge has made every effort to trace copyright holders and to obtain permission to publish extracts. Any omissions brought to our attention will be remedied in future editions.

Chapter one

Texts and contexts

A framework

All academic subjects have methods of enquiry which need to be employed, methods which are based upon certain theoretical frameworks. English is no exception. This book is based on the central idea that when you study English at an advanced level, your reading of texts will be more thorough and sophisticated if you approach it through a clear framework. In doing this, your critical responses will come from a methodical approach, just as happens in other subjects you study.

This should not mean that reading becomes a chore, yet another activity burdened by complex jargon and terminology. What it should mean is that you are more receptive to different ways of looking at texts, and that you get more from them by realising that their meanings are not fixed. Note here that the word 'meanings' has deliberately been used in the plural, to emphasise that you are not searching for one meaning that is correct, but for the many meanings that are possible.

Having a theoretical framework for your study of literature, far from cramping your style, in fact gives you the freedom to look at texts in more varied and creative ways.

For most of the twentieth century, advanced reading at sixth form involved the reading of 'great works' from Literature; there were no English language courses at sixth form and no courses which allowed the study of language alongside that of literature. Generally speaking, students read works by 'great' authors, chosen by their teachers who then guided them towards an understanding of what these books were supposedly 'about'. This meant that the content of the texts was always seen as far more important than the processes of reading them. It also meant that studying literature was a rather passive process.

This way of looking at texts is now challenged by critics, teachers and students, who argue that the processes of writing and reading require a more rigorous, coherent analysis. This in turn frees the student to be a more active participant in the process, sharing the reading rather than receiving it from someone else.

When old ideas are being challenged by new methods, there is inevitably conflict and resentment, making it necessary, often, for writers and teachers to declare where they stand. This will be done in this opening chapter.

Task

The four numbered sections below give you a flavour of how approaches to reading have developed and changed. For the sake of clarity and simplicity, each section has a paragraph marked 'Then' and another marked 'Now'. The first paragraph looks at how texts have often been read in the past; the second offers a more modern view, which this book encourages you to take as you work your way through it. As you read through these four sections, ask yourself the following questions:

1   With which of the approaches to reading are you familiar?
2   What methods did you use/were you encouraged to use at earlier stages of your education?
3   This book is clearly advocating the methods marked 'Now'. What do you think?

Literature and reality

Then Authors, it was sometimes assumed, wrote about and reflected an absolute thing called 'reality'. They put meaning and reality into their texts, and if the readers were intelligent enough, and helped by a teacher who could show them how to see it, they would be able to see this reality presented to them. This led to the idea that characters in books were also 'real'. An example of this, which is sometimes still given to students, is in *Wuthering Heights*: 'Is Heathcliff a

2

hero or a villain?' Stated like this, it removes the author and the reader from the equation. It even removes the idea that this is a character in a novel, while also suggesting that Heathcliff must be either a hero or villain, but not a mixture of both.

In some cases, this concept of real characters led to the idea that they even have lives outside the books in which they appear. One of the best-known products of this bizarre idea is the work of the critic A.C. Bradley in which he speculates on issues such as 'Did Emilia suspect Iago?' or 'Did Lady Macbeth really faint?'

Now   There is no such thing as absolute, objective reality. All use of language involves the language user and the language receiver in a relationship – and relationships are complex things, viewed differently by all involved. There can therefore be no such thing as objective 'reality' reflected by a great author and understood by a reader. Instead, all things are relative, and the best way to study a text is to explore it with an open mind, using various approaches.

Literature and genius

Then   Writers, especially dead ones, were often made out to be geniuses; they somehow rose above common mortality and the social and cultural issues of their time, to produce works which are timeless in their meaning and significance. Shakespeare is still, of course, often held up as the classic example of true genius at work. In British exam syllabuses, decreed by Government, Shakespeare stands in a category all by himself, outside the requirements of time or genre. He is seen neither as a dramatist, nor as an Elizabethan – he is simply Shakespeare, simply the best, better than all the rest. This means that the variable qualities of his plays have often gone unquestioned.

Now   Texts are produced by authors who live in the political and social world of their time, and we gain a better understanding of their works by taking these contexts into account. It is sometimes wrongly suggested that texts are somehow self-contained, existing in a world of their own and so free from outside influences. This in turn leads to the idea that some authors are geniuses who manage to operate outside the world the rest of us inhabit. Writers, including Shakespeare, are often very skilled in their craft, but they are not superhuman.

Literature and the reader

Then   The role of the reader, one part of the relationship described in 'Literature and reality' above, was often ignored. This meant that texts were seen to be independent of their readers. They sat on a shelf with their meaning already encoded, waiting to be picked up by a reader who would try to break the code and extract the meaning. Reading would be a very limited, and limiting, activity if this were the case.

If texts were seen to have a fixed and permanent meaning which did not change, either with time or with different readers, then this in turn led to the idea that society would be a better place if everyone at school was forced to read the works of 'great' authors. These texts would contain clear and unchanging moral lessons, which students would then put into effect in their own lives. This view is still held in some political quarters.

Now   *The Merchant of Venice,* with its anti-semitism, or *The Taming of the Shrew* , with its sexism, surely need to be challenged as examples of good morality at work. A text cannot have an existence independent of its readers, who recreate the text through bringing their own culturally-conditioned views and attitudes to bear on it. Each reader recreates the text as it is read – and re-read – because no reading is ever the same. This makes readers active, vital participants in the reading process, rather than mere passive recipients of accepted ideas. If readers are actively creating new meanings, then logically this means that the text cannot contain any single fixed permanent meaning. An extension of this is that books may encourage readers to consider moral issues, but books are not in themselves going to change social behaviour, or make people behave more morally.

Literature and interpretation

Then   Students were often told that there is no right answer, that as long as you have an opinion, then it is valid. Literature, it was claimed, is all about individual personal response, which the reader's mind intuitively produces when it is in contact with great texts. This at first sight might seem to contradict what has been said about encoded meanings in 'Literature and the reader' above; the idea of individual response only paid lip-service to freedom of thought. What it really implied is that texts have a timeless meaning and significance, which is only reached by paying careful attention to a teacher

4

and other critics who have already worked out what it all means. Your opinion was only valid if you read by the rules.

Now Although it is agreed that there is no single right 'answer' in literary analysis, it cannot be accepted that any *opinion* is valid. Just as other academic subjects require the careful application and evaluation of different theories, so does reading. The result of careful study is not so much opinion, but *informed judgement.* Applying to texts different aspects of a reading framework will produce many different ideas, interpretations, meanings. Weighing these up, and deciding which ones you respond to in particular, is what needs to be encouraged – but this involves rather more method than merely having an opinion.

Summary

The governing principle of this book is to suggest that it is possible to approach texts, including literary texts, in a variety of ways which can be explained and then applied. How you responded to the first two questions about your earlier reading will to some extent determine your response to the third. You may feel that you are already acquainted with many of the ideas that are marked as modern. On the other hand you may feel annoyed that methods and assumptions that you have worked with before are now being challenged; that things are suddenly being made difficult. Far from making reading more difficult, looking at contexts can provide a framework which allows you, the reader, to work out your own ideas and responses without feeling that there is somehow a right answer out there which only the privileged few can access. This should make your study of English more varied, more challenging, and ultimately more fun.

The next part of this opening chapter introduces a framework based upon the idea of contexts.

The word 'contexts': the assessment objectives for rewritten Advanced Level courses, which will begin the new millennium, talk of students 'studying the contexts in which texts were written'. The word 'context' has had different uses in the study of English, and it is worth looking at these first.

For many years the word 'context' was used to describe a particular sort of exercise in English studies. Students were given a small part of a larger text they had already studied, and were then asked a series of questions on it. It was a sort of quiz or puzzle, because essentially they had to recognise whereabouts in the text it came, what it showed about the plot or action at that point and possibly what it showed about the text as a whole. The questions that were asked usually focused on behaviour of characters, the themes that were being explored and something called the 'style' of the passage.

In the A Level assessment objectives, and in this book too, the word 'context' is used in a different way from that mentioned in the previous paragraph. Like all words involving the root 'text', 'context' originates from the idea of weaving together, as in 'textile'. *The New Oxford Dictionary*, published in 1998, defines context as 'the circumstances that form the setting for an event, statement or idea, and in terms of which it can be fully understood and assessed'. In other words, instead of looking at small bits of a text in predictable ways, this book will suggest that exploring context involves much bigger issues – the 'circumstances' that contribute both to its production by the author and to its reception by the reader. Context refers to what goes *with* a text, rather than what is *in* it.

You should note at this point that in the A Level assessment objectives, the word 'contexts' is in the plural. So too is the word 'circumstances' in the New Oxford definition quoted above. This deliberate use of plurals is important for you to recognise. The plurals suggest that when reading texts we are looking for more than a single perspective, rooted in a single cause.

This book uses the idea of contexts while it explores ideas around the writing and reading of texts. Listed below are five broad strands of context that will be explored through a range of texts and ideas and with questions which give you some idea of what is involved in each strand. As you work through the book, you, as reader, will be asked how the answers to these questions affect the way you view the texts under discussion.

Although these strands may seem unusual or complex at this stage, do not worry; each chapter will return to these central ideas about context and your understanding of them will develop as you work through the book.

A context framework

The writer's context

1   What do we know about the writer's life, values, assumptions, gender, race, class, sexual orientation etc.?

2   What do we know about the values and assumptions prevalent in the culture in which the writer lived? How was the writer influenced by these values and to what extent did the writer challenge them?
3   What political/economic issues were important at the time?

The text's context

1   What is its publishing history? For example: are there different versions; is it read in translation; was it originally serialised; is it part of a larger text such as a newspaper or anthology?
2   What sources contributed to it?
3   What is the text's relationship to other texts; does it, for instance, echo the language of another text, the ideas of another text?
4   What is its history of performance and what audience and/or readers has it had over time?
5   What previous critical reviews has it received and how do they affect the way we view the text now?

The reader's context

1   What is your previous reading experience?
2   How do your values, assumptions, gender, race, class, age, sexual orientation etc. affect the way you read the text?
3   How are your views shaped by the political and economic issues of your time?
4   How are your views shaped by the values and assumptions of the culture in which you live?

The readings context

1   How do different critical schools respond to this text?
2   How can different critical theories and methods be applied to the text?
3   How is the text ambiguous in its meanings?
4   What is left unsaid in the text?

The language context

1   What generic conventions does the text follow, and how does the reader recognise them?
2   How is the text's narrative organised?
3   How do various linguistic features affect the way we read the text?
4   In what ways can we approach the question 'How does this text work?'

All of the above questions form ways to approach the single question 'What does this text mean?'

It is important at this stage to stress that these are not listed in any sort of hierarchy. All texts are subject to enquiry from the standpoints of all the contexts listed above. As was noted earlier, when discussing contexts, we are looking at plurality. This means that there is no single right response when studying texts and it is possible, indeed preferable, to see that there are many different ways that a text can be read and discussed. This means that you are not looking for one solution when you read and study texts, but for lots of different ways of approaching and responding to them.

Conclusion

This opening chapter has introduced some ideas which may be new to you, and has suggested some theoretical ways of looking at texts. It has also challenged some traditional views about how to study literature. Above all it has said that you, the reader, are as important as the author of the text you are reading. The next chapter begins the task of putting the theory into practice.

Chapter two

Texts and contexts

Whose dog are you?

In the last chapter you were introduced to the idea of context. In this chapter the idea is expanded further with a short practical activity to work on. To help you develop your understanding of the idea of context, you are given a task, followed by a commentary. You can either complete the task first, and then look at the commentary, or you can use the commentary to help you with your answers.

Task

Read the following poem carefully a number of times; then work at the questions which follow.

Text *Epigram*

Epigram Engraved on the Collar of a Dog which I Gave to His Royal Highness

I am his Highness' dog at Kew:
Pray tell me, sir, whose dog are you?

Alexander Pope

Either individually or in a group, write:

1   briefly what you understand this poem to be about;

2   a list of questions that arise from your reading of the poem, the answers to which you would find helpful when analysing this poem. They may include words you do not understand, factual detail you would find helpful etc.

Commentary

When given these tasks, one group of students came up with the following questions:

1   What is an epigram?
2   Who is 'I' and 'you' in the poem? Is 'I' in the title different from 'I' in the poem?
3   What exactly was given to his Highness?
4   Who does 'sir' refer to?
5   What is Kew? Who was His Royal Highness?
6   When was this poem written and do we know anything about why Pope may have written it?

An epigram is defined as 'a short poem, especially a satirical one, which has a clever and witty ending'. In the title to his poem, Pope spells out that it belongs to a certain **genre**. Looking at the genre of a text is one way of thinking about its content and purpose. By giving the poem the label of an epigram, Pope is stating that the poem is satirical in purpose and he hopes to amuse the reader. Such a long title to such a short poem is also to comic effect.

This epigram is not only brief, it is also written in a rhyming couplet. A rhyming couplet is a term used to describe two lines of poetry which rhyme, and whose sense is usually complete. Because of the rhythm, and the growing anticipation of the rhyme which completes the couplet, it can be argued that the greatest weight or emphasis in a couplet comes with the last word, especially if it is monosyllabic. Here the last word is 'you'. This leads us to look at pronouns in the poem, but later the commentary will return to the importance of this final word.

Pronouns are words which are normally substituted for nouns, such as 'I', 'You', etc. Pronouns require what is technically called **pronoun reference**; they make sense because they refer to something that has already been named. The problem here is that the pronouns cannot easily be placed in their reference. Who is the 'I' of the title, and is it the same 'I' who appears in the first line of the poem? Who is the 'you' in the last line of the poem? It seems to refer to the word 'sir', but who this 'sir' is remains vague. There are many possible ways of looking at these pronouns and that is deliberate – Pope actually wants the reader to be uncertain. He has deliberately created **ambiguity**.

In looking at genre, effects of verse sounds and structure, and pronouns, you are focusing on the linguistic features of the poem – part of **the language context**. When coming to a text 'cold', without the benefit of extra information, it is likely that your first responses, your first ways into the text will be linguistic, drawing also on your previous experience as a reader of texts.

Another way of thinking about the pronouns, and another part of **the language context**, is to explore what **narrative structure** is being used here. It seems unlikely that the same narrative 'I' is being used in the title as in the poem itself: in the title it could be the author himself, or a fictional persona invented by the author; in the poem it could be the 'voice' of the dog wearing the collar. We must then ask who is reading the text, who is being addressed by it when the word 'you' is used? In the final reckoning, of course, it is you the actual reader, but there is also a created reader here, an imagined fictional reader who meets the dog and reads its collar. Who could this be? Someone who comes across the dog at Kew? Or even the King himself who does, after all, own the dog?

Because of the various possibilities, this seems rather complex – as narrative in texts can be. It often helps to show the process in a tabular form:

◎   real author (Pope)
◎   invents persona ('I' of title)
◎   who invents a fictional voice ('I' of poem; the dog)
◎   which speaks to an imagined reader ('you' who reads the collar; king? courtiers?)
◎   which is read by the real reader ('you' who works out the real point).

Ultimately, the real author is communicating with the real reader, but the way this is done is vital to the way the message is received. Just as it can be wrong to assume that the 'I' who narrates a story is actually the author, when it can be a fictional character, so it can be wrong to assume that the story is addressed directly to the real reader, when it can be addressed to a fictional reader or readers.

Two useful terms to use when talking about narrative like this distinguish the **narrator** who tells the story from the **narratee** who reads it. The narrator is an invented 'voice' who speaks the text. The narratee is an invented reader for whom the text is supposedly written. A good way of understanding the idea of the narratee is to look at advertising. Car adverts often construct a narratee with a life-style far removed from that led by most of us, and cosmetic adverts feature people who are young, sexy and attractive in a way that most of us are not. The companies paying for the adverts hope that the real readers will be seduced by the images of a created world that we do not really inhabit.

Returning to the text of the poem, what is it, exactly, that Pope claims to have given the King? Is it a collar with an epigram on it? Or is it a dog he gave the King, which has since been fitted with a collar? Both readings are possible within the deliberately ambiguous grammar of the title. If Pope gave the King the collar, then he has presumably also written the words for it – but not on it, because he has a co-conspirator in the engraver. If Pope gave the King the dog, though, then Pope has been rather less cheeky; someone else, unnamed, has written the script. But anyway, do we really believe that Pope gives the King a gift at all? Pope, we must assume, is telling a fictional story, albeit one surrounded by all sorts of ambiguity; and just because an event is written in a piece of text, it does not mean it actually happened. Does all this ambiguity and wit protect Pope from accusations of going too far, or is the ambiguity itself a challenge to the King and his authority? It is impossible to answer these questions at this stage, but some research into Pope's life and times might clarify the issues; in other words we might turn to **the writer's context** for help.

The final two questions listed by the students (see above) also ask for help with **the writer's context** of the poem, for information about the author and his time which might help a modern reader who does not necessarily understand the references. Kew refers to Kew Gardens, at the time (the eighteenth century) a fashionable place for the rich and favoured to be seen. Its house and gardens would have been peopled by courtiers and favourites, people whom Pope both disliked and perhaps envied. Pope is known as a satirical poet who mocked the pretensions and follies especially of those people with power and influence. This was in part because he himself was excluded from the élite cliques, not least because he was a Catholic at a time when they were viewed with considerable suspicion.

It was noted earlier that the final word of the poem, and the one that perhaps carries most weight, is the word 'you', which itself refers back to the word 'sir' in the same line. As we might expect in a poem which carries so much ambiguity, the reference for this word carries a number of possibilities, involving both fictional narratees and the real reader.

1   Within the fictional framework of the poem, 'you' could refer to the courtiers of Kew who find the dog and read its collar.
2   It could refer to the King who owns the dog, and so is in the best position to read the collar.
3   It could refer to other dogs who meet this one. This sounds strange – dogs cannot read; but nor can dogs talk, so within the idea of a talking dog you can also have reading dogs. Many fables, after all, depict animals who behave like humans.
4   The 'you' could refer to you the reader of the poem, someone outside the fictional framework. Women could argue that because of the word 'sir', they are excluded from this reference; it is only male readers who are addressed – unless, that is, you take the word 'sir' to include both genders, as the word 'man' once did and still sometimes does. Certainly the King was male, and so were those courtiers with any power and influence. This reference to the word 'you' would be part of **the reader's context**; how do you respond to this potential reference to yourself, and how do you respond to its implications with regard to gender? Is it refer-ring historically to men because they were the only figures with power, or do you see it as relevant today because men still exercise power, and behave in a certain way once they have it? The answers you give will depend upon your own construction of the world around you.

So far, then, this poem has been subjected to analysis using various theoretical methods. Putting all the evidence and questions together, and coming to **the readings context**, Pope's satirical epigram seems to suggest that followers of the King (and even maybe the King himself) are like lap-dogs, without any individuality or real value; they have sacrificed their integrity for apparent power and influence, but at the same time belittled themselves in the process. Behind the apparently jokey surface lies a cutting edge. The fact that the poem contains ambiguity, that its meaning is open to debate, should not worry you as a reader – this can be seen as a positive virtue.

13

The poem also has a resonance today, well ahead of its historical context. In these days of cabinet bust-ups and political in-fighting it is still relevant to ask questions of those who seek power.

Conclusion

In this chapter you have seen how a writer's choice of genre, structure and language has led to several possible meanings and interpretations. The poem can convey something different today than in Pope's time, and meanings we find in the poem are open-ended, shaped by several examples of ambiguity at the heart of the poem.

This one very short poem has illustrated several methods that can be used when investigating texts. Four of the contexts mentioned in the original framework have been explored; the exception, **the text's context** – especially where and how the poem was first published – could be researched by using reference books on Pope. Each of the contexts opens up some useful insights, and when taken together they all add to our understanding of how the poem works. This process will now be used to look at some more substantial texts.

Chapter three

Texts and contexts

Raising the *Titanic*

Many of the questions posed in the 'framework' in Chapter 1 of this book will now be explored by looking at a number of texts which are connected thematically by a single historical event, the sinking of the *Titanic*. The way different authors, writing at different times for different purposes, treat this event will help you to understand some of the key ideas surrounding contexts.

The *Titanic* left Southampton on its maiden voyage on 10 April 1912. It sank on the night of 14 April, having collided with an iceberg. The story of this ship has formed the basis of a number of written texts, as well as countless films. The 1997 film, directed by James Cameron, won numerous Oscars and was a huge box-office success.

Writers of texts about the *Titanic*, and makers of films about it, have always had a great deal of information available to them. The longer that time has elapsed, the more information there is to work with, as the story has been constantly retold and reanalysed. What writers choose to focus on will tell you something about their own interests in the story and also about cultural values prevalent at the time of writing.

Task

Imagine you are going to write a short story based on the events surrounding the *Titanic*, but like all writers you need an angle on your story. How might each of the following pieces of information give you an angle from which to approach the story? Take each in turn.

1   The ship was part-owned by the American millionaire J.P. Morgan. Just before departure, he cancelled his reservation on the ship, claiming ill-health. Fifty-four others cancelled reservations at the last minute.

    The ship look-outs, who were watching for icebergs, had no binoculars – these had disappeared somewhere between Belfast, where the ship was built, and Southampton, where it set sail.

2   There were 337 first-class passengers (mainly American); 271 second-class (mainly British); 712 third-class (nearly all of whom were immigrants from Italy, Ireland, Armenia, Russia, China and the Lebanon; 123 Lebanese passengers were drowned).

3   Unlike most modern disasters, this one happened slowly, in that it took over two hours for the ship to sink from the moment it hit the iceberg.

4   Although there is no documentary evidence of the ship ever being called 'unsinkable', there was enormous pride in its luxury and design. The first-class areas were fabulously decorated and resembled a huge hotel. The writer Osbert Sitwell called the episode 'a symbol of the approaching fate of Western civilisation'. The ship weighed 46,000 tons; the iceberg something like 500,000.

Responses

The following are some suggestions made by students working at this task. There are obviously no right answers, but compare your ideas with those below.

1   This information might lead a modern writer to see a conspiracy behind the ship's sinking; did the owners know something in advance? This will be understood by contemporary audiences who are used to a culture of corruption among the rich and powerful, and the exposure of this corruption in documentaries and investigative journalism.

2   It would be difficult to write about the *Titanic* without seeing its physical structure – different decks for different statuses, with the first class on top – as an example of how social class operates, and how the rich manipulate the poor. The most recent film, which was made in America, romanticised and at the same time

blurred these differences by having the central fictional couple played as poor boy loves rich girl.

The third class, especially those who did not originate in America or Western Europe, have largely been ignored in tellings of the story. A version of events written by a Lebanese person, for example, would be very different in its focus, and would be likely to see the story in a different political context.

3   One problem facing a modern writer would be the fact that everyone knows the outline of the story, and the end cannot be altered – the ship must sink. Additionally, the plot is likely to have three parts: some sense of the journey before the iceberg; a description of what happened during the actual sinking; and some sense of afterwards. The structure of the story would need to be worked out carefully.

4   This information might lead you to take a more symbolic view of the story: that it represented more than just a disaster in 1912, but an example of how men and their technology can be defeated by nature, or by higher powers.

The responses above, and others that you may have come up with, show some of the issues which influence the way texts are written and also, therefore, the way they are read because readers too come to the text with their own ideas and influences. We will now look at how some authors have approached the sinking of the *Titanic*.

Thomas Hardy   *The Convergence of the Twain*

The first text to be looked at here will be Thomas Hardy's poem *The Convergence of the Twain*. This poem was written for a 'Dramatic and Operatic Matinée in aid of the *Titanic* Disaster Fund' soon after the disaster. Hardy had two friends on the ship who did not survive the tragedy.

Task

Given the information above, what expectations would you have as a reader of this poem? What expectations would the audience at the 'matinée' have had?

Make brief notes before reading the poem. When you have read the poem twice, compare your responses to the poem with your prior expectations. Then read the commentary which follows and compare its ideas with yours.

17

Text *The Convergence of the Twain*
       (lines on the loss of the *Titanic*)

I

In a solitude of the sea
Deep from human vanity,
And the Pride of Life that planned her, stilly couches she.

II

Steel chambers, late the pyres
Of her salamandrine fires,
Cold currents thrid, and turn to rhythmic tidal lyres.

III

Over the mirrors meant
To glass the opulent
The sea-worm crawls – grotesque, slimed, dumb, indifferent.

IV

Jewels in joy designed
To ravish the sensuous mind
Lie lightless, all their sparkles bleared and black and blind.

V

Dim moon-eyed fishes near
Gaze at the gilded gear
And query: 'What does this vaingloriousness down here?'

VI

Well: while was fashioning
This creature of cleaving wing,
The Immanent Will that stirs and urges everything

VII

Prepared a sinister mate
For her – so gaily great –
A Shape of Ice, for the time far and dissociate.

VIII

And as the smart ship grew
In stature, grace, and hue,
In shadowy silent distance grew the Iceberg too.

IX

Alien they seemed to be
No mortal eye could see
The intimate welding of their later history,

X

Or sign that they were bent
By paths coincident
On being anon twin halves of one august event,

XI

Till the Spinner of the Years
Said 'Now!' And each one hears,
And consummation comes, and jars two hemispheres.

Commentary

It is not often that a poem has such a clear factual basis; it is about an actual historical event and was written for a highly specific purpose. Our expectations of the poem are probably that it will ask the reader to sympathise with the victims, that it will have a sense of loss and wasted life, that it will ask why such things happen. There is a good role model for this response. The poet – and Catholic priest – Gerard Manley Hopkins wrote a long poem called *The Wreck of the Deutschland* about a ship which sank in 1875, drowning five nuns in the process. Hopkins viewed the event as an example of the ultimate mystery, power and wonder of the God he believed in.

One way of looking at texts is to describe what they are not, and this poem is an excellent example. A useful term to describe what a text could contain, but does not, is **absence**. There will be a number of things which may well have puzzled you on a first reading, not least in understanding the meaning of some of the words, but the major surprises are likely to be consistent with those of other readers.

A group of students working at this task came up with the following list of things the poem does not do:

1   It does not apparently express any grief.
2   It does not try to imagine the extent of the panic/chaos/ suffering.
3   It does not seem to express much blame, just resignation.
4   It does not say anything about those recently bereaved, including those attending the matinée service.
5   It does not seem to expect the reader to feel any emotion.

Task

The poem, then, has not stood up to our expectations. Nonetheless, it is saying something, so this second task will explore what the poem does do, bearing in mind that we came to it expecting something rather different.

Re-read the poem at least twice and prepare notes on the following:

1   What contrasts between pairs of opposites can you find in the poem?
2   What do you notice about the design and structure of the poem?
3   One **metaphor**, or comparison, in particular dominates the poem. Trace its progress through the poem, by noting where it occurs. The last line gives you a good idea of what the metaphor is.

Commentary

The title of the poem contains the word 'Twain', an archaic word meaning two. In the most obvious pairing, there is the ship or 'she' and the iceberg or her 'sinister mate'. There are many other potential pairs in the poem, however, which contrast the ship before and after the sinking. Among them are these:

fire and water
light and dark
reflection and non-reflection
sparkle and dullness
solitude and humanity

Others compare the ship and the iceberg:

> opulence and slime
> noise and silence
> near and far
> cleaving wing and shape of ice

Using the last two as an example, there is a constant sense of contrast in the poem, in this case between the streamlined ship which will surge through the water and the mere lumpen shape of the clumsy iceberg. As the first line of the verse IX says, 'Alien they seemed to be'. Both groups of contrasts deliberately highlight extremes of difference, whether it be the splendour of the ship now lost to the Atlantic, or the 'gaily great' ship in all its glory compared to the dull and lumbering iceberg. The extremes of difference between the two, yet the fact that they come together, make the event 'august' – striking (in both senses of the word) but not emotional. The reader is asked to respond intellectually to what happened rather than emotionally.

This leads to a comparison not yet mentioned: that between man who was 'fashioning' the ship, both building it and making it fashionable, and the Immanent Will (later called the Spinner of the Years) which was 'preparing' the iceberg. Readers familiar with Hardy, especially his novels, will know that he frequently refers to fate, to forces outside man's control, forces which lead to tragedy of some sort.

This then is one aspect of his response: humanity thinks it is in control but it isn't really. The wonderful man-made ship is no match for the lumpen iceberg.

It can be argued that each verse of this poem looks rather like a ship, with the third line of each verse being the hull. Even if you find this a bit far-fetched, you will have noticed other distinctive features of the poem's structure. Each of the three lines of each verse rhyme, with a number of the rhymes created through polysyllabic words – opulent/indifferent. (Polysyllabic refers to words with several syllables in them; rhymes in poems tend to involve words with one or two syllables.)

There are many alliterative phrases which also contribute to the overall **phonological** effect. (Phonology involves the analysis of the way words sound.) Each of the first five verses is very self-contained, ending with a stop, and the actual numbering of the verses also seems to suggest that they are self-contained. Using roman numerals gives an old-fashioned touch to a poem written about a contemporary event, perhaps suggesting that although this is a poem about a specific event, it is also a poem about the way people have always behaved.

The unusual opening to verse VI: 'Well:' sounds a very different note; it sounds distinctly conversational after what has gone before, especially words like 'vaingloriouness'. What it also does is to break the text in two, as all accounts of the *Titanic* seem to do. Here, though, Hardy reverses the usual order of before and after – this time it is after that comes first, followed by before, with the last two lines being the 'Now!' of the actual collision.

The last line is a good starting point for looking at the poem's most important metaphor. The word 'consummation' – literally meaning sexual intercourse – suggests that the ship and the iceberg do not so much collide as have sex together. From the start of the poem the ship has been called 'she'; we may not have particularly noticed this on first reading because often, ships are gendered in this way. We must also remember that the *Titanic* was on its maiden voyage – as far as the sea was concerned it was a virgin. The iceberg being described as 'mate' (a ship-mate?) completes the idea of the ship and the iceberg having a relationship, although they seem to be 'alien'. They are, as was noted above, no match for each other.

Looking again at the last line, there is another word which describes the sexual act between the two; it 'jars'. This is not consenting sex, but rape. However you interpret this idea – in human sexual terms, or in terms of fate hurting humanity – the image is one of violent and sudden force. This contrasts with the 'stilly'ness of the opening verses, but they too contain gendered images. There is a strong sense that human vanity contributed to all this, and that the human vanity is presented as female; the mirrors and jewels were and still are part of the traditional representation of women's appearance.

So, this discussion of the poem ends where it began, focusing on contrast and duality, and suggesting that however it is read it makes for unusual and, for the matinée audience, uncomfortable reading.

This discussion has touched upon all five of the reading contexts mentioned earlier: Hardy's previous works, his attitude to women, his values expressed in the poem are part of **the writer's context**. As readers, meanwhile, whether or not you accept the interpretation above will depend in part upon your own values, **the reader's context**. The publishing history of the text, its being part of a memorial performance is part of **the text's context.** The structure, appearance and phonology of the poem are part of its **language context**. Finally its multiple meanings, with a particular emphasis on metaphor and its representation of gender are all part of the readings context. You will notice, though, that the commentary on the poem does not work through these contexts one by one, as though they are somehow separate.

Beryl Bainbridge   *Every Man for Himself*

One of the ways we have looked at Hardy's poem was to consider its effect on one particular audience – those who attended the memorial event, including some who had lost family and friends in the disaster. As modern readers, we have had to consider a previous set of readers too. This is obviously not the case when we consider a text published much more recently, especially when it is a work of fiction.

Different questions have to be considered. Some of these could be:

1   What is there 'new' to say about such a well-known story?
2   How can a reader be kept interested in a narrative whose conclusion is already known?
3   How much of the text will be about 'before' the iceberg, and how much about 'after'?
4   A modern re-working of an historical event must say at least as much about modern times as about past times: what will be said, and how?

To put some of these questions to the test, the following extract is taken from the novel *Every Man for Himself* by Beryl Bainbridge (1996).

The title *Every Man For Himself* refers to the notion of 'women and children first, then every man for himself,' which was supposed to be the order of events when abandoning a sinking ship. In highlighting only the last part of the statement, Bainbridge is potentially also referring to wider issues about the lives led by her fictional characters, both before and after the ship sets sail.

Bainbridge uses some of the 'real' people in the historical event as hooks for the story, but the central characters are completely fictional. Thus the novel is narrated by an imaginary young American called Morgan, an orphan originally, but vaguely related to the 'real' J.P. Morgan, the millionaire and owner of the *Titanic*. J.P. Morgan has financed Morgan through life, which included a stint at Harland and Wolff, the shipbuilder. Morgan survives the disaster.

The novel is divided up into accounts of each day. Bainbridge weaves in various parts of the known history of the trip, and of the ship's opulent design, but these details are only in passing – the real hub of the narrative involves the lives of a small group of first-class characters. Morgan knows quite a bit about the ship, but not much about life – and nothing at all about sex. Through his naïve eyes we see a morally bankrupt bunch of people who are, unknown to them, living out their final days.

Only in the final part of the novel do we reach the disaster. The following extract comes at the point when the iceberg hits. Charlie Melchett, Hopper and Ginsberg are part of Morgan's group of friends, although Ginsberg is not much liked. Smith the captain, Andrews the designer, Lady Duff Gordon and Bruce Ismay were all 'real'.

Task

Read the following extract carefully. Prepare answers/responses to the following questions:

1   What do you notice about the description of the actual collision?
2   What details does Morgan, as the created narrator, give the 'created' reader? How do you as the 'real' reader react to these?
3   Remembering that Morgan is a survivor of the disaster, what do you notice about the way events and time are sequenced here?
4   Can you find any ideas in the extract which are similar to Hardy's in his poem?

Do not refer to the commentary which follows until you have completed your answers.

Text   *Every Man for Himself*

They had been gone no more than ten minutes – Ginsberg had ordered a whisky and Charlie and I had just won three tricks in succession – when suddenly the room juddered; the lights flickered and Ginsberg's cigarette case, which sat at his elbow, jolted to the floor. It was the sound accompanying the juddering that startled us, a long drawn-out tearing, like a vast length of calico slowly ripping apart. Melchett said, 'We're in collision with another ship,' and with that we threw down our cards, ran to the doors, sprinted through the Palm Court and out on to the deck. A voice called, 'We've bumped an iceberg – there it goes,' but though I peered into the darkness I could see nothing. From somewhere forward we heard laughter, voices excitedly shouting. Coming to the starboard rail I looked down on to the well of the third class recreation area; there were chunks of ice spilling and sliding in every direction, all shapes and sizes, glittering under the light of the foremast. Steerage passengers, most in their ragged night-clothes, were chucking it at each other as though playing snow-balls. Hopper raced off to go down there and join in the fun. Charlie and I found it too cold to linger and hurried back indoors. A dozen or so men had poured out of the smoke-room and were milling about the foyer, pestering the stewards for information. Astor was there, still dressed but without his tie, leaning down to shout into the ear of Seefax who had been woken from sleep in the library and now sat on the staircase with his stick raised like a weapon. Everyone had a different explanation for what-ever it was that had jarred the ship; Ginsberg swore we had lost a propeller, but what did he know?

We couldn't resume our game until Hopper returned, which he did quite soon, triumphantly carrying a lump of ice in his handkerchief. He thrust it under my nose and it smelt rank, a bit like a sliver of rotten mack-erel. He dropped it into Ginsberg's whisky when the poor devil wasn't looking. We must have played for another ten minutes, by which time Hopper said he'd had enough. Remembering Andrews' injunction that I should read while others slept, I decided to spend an hour in the library. I was crossing the foyer when the man himself swept past on his way to the stairs. I didn't think he'd seen me but he said quite distinctly, 'Follow me. You may be needed.'

Commentary

The moment the ship hits the iceberg is anticipated by all engaged in a narrative about the *Titanic* voyage, whether it be on film or in a novel. This is unusual in a narrative; usually we want to know what will happen, as well as when and how. Here we know what will happen, and in a sense when and how too. For Hardy the collision was a climax, which jarred, but Bainbridge establishes where she will focus our attention by underplaying the impact, as described by her narrator Morgan.

Look carefully at the first sentence of this extract. The first indi-cation of the collision comes with the word 'juddered', but this is only in the second half of an already long sentence, after we have been told about characters disappearing, drinks being ordered, card tricks won. The verbs which describe the impact are all subdued in their force – along with 'juddered', there is 'flickered' and the slightly stronger 'jolted'. The impact, such as it is, is shrouded in small detail – cigarette

25

cases, cards, drinks. An unidentified voice tells them that they have 'bumped' an iceberg. Accompanying the sense of touch comes a description of sound; although this startles them, it is likened to 'calico slowly ripping apart' – the tearing of metal becomes the ripping of dress fabric.

At this stage of the story, a reader would expect short sentences and paragraphs to convey the expected force of the event. Instead there is an unusually long paragraph, with 'laughter' and many different explanations, all in some sense missing the real point.

This first paragraph means that the reader knows better than the narrator Morgan, who remains stuck in a world where personal vanity, how others see you, is constantly highlighted. Morgan is at the very centre of his own world and his own concern at how others see him, but Bainbridge places him only on the edge of what really matters. He expects his audience of the 'created' reader to understand his concerns; he thinks that we, like him and his cronies, are interested in the social subtleties of polite behaviour. As real readers, though, with the full knowledge of what is 'really' happening, we are shocked at his complacency.

For this effect to work, we have to have a **chronological narrative** which excludes any sense of hindsight on the part of Morgan. Surely anyone narrating the story would comment on how deceived they were, would, with the survivor's benefit of knowing the full story, break the strict chronology and reflect on events from a different perspective. Instead, this extract with its references to intervals of 'ten minutes' keeps strictly to chronological sequence. This allows Bainbridge to highlight the complacency of the ruling class, which literally 'looked down' on the steerage class 'in their ragged night-clothes' and believed itself immune to disaster.

It will now be clear that Hardy and Bainbridge do have some things in common; both are writing about vanity, both comment on human smugness in the face of disaster, and both create narratives which are unusual in the way that they approach the story. As was seen with the Hardy poem, your responses, along with the ideas in this commentary, have explored different contexts: in this case Bainbridge's ideas concerning the socially privileged; your own knowledge as the reader; where this extract fits in the whole novel; its use of language and what it ultimately 'means' to its readers.

G.B. Shaw   *Some Unmentioned Morals*

George Bernard Shaw is best known as a playwright. He was also a
journalist and commentator, and in May 1912 he wrote an article
decrying the mythologising that had already begun around the story
of the *Titanic*. In the article entitled *Some Unmentioned Morals*, he
attacked the way the story was being reported in the English press,
saying that the sinking of the ship was being viewed as a triumph for
the English nation, when it was in fact nothing of the sort.

His article itself became the object of a bitter dispute with the
writer Sir Arthur Conan Doyle, who said 'it is a pitiful sight to see a
man of undoubted genius using his gifts in order to misrepresent and
decry his own people'. Shaw, who was Irish by birth, was unlikely to
feel that the English were his 'own people', but far from 'misrepre-
senting' the English, he urges that they are best served by openly
accepting what really happened.

Conan Doyle's use of the word 'misrepresentation' highlights
how the two authors disagreed. Representation involves the way
something is portrayed, and that portrayal is influenced by all the
contextual factors outlined in the first chapter of this book. When
Conan Doyle challenges Shaw's 'misrepresentation', he is in effect
claiming that there is a single, 'true' way of portraying what
happened, and that Shaw is wrong to challenge this. At a time, just
before the First World War, when nationalism was a potent political
force, Shaw urges his readers to look behind the surface representations of national glory and see a very different story.

Task

Read the edited extract from Shaw's article and answer the following
question:

How does Shaw organise his attack on the English press and its
representation of the story?

Text   *Some Unmentioned Morals*

Why is it that the effect of a sensational catastrophe on a modern nation is
to cast it into transports, not of weeping, not of prayer, not of sympathy
with the bereaved nor congratulation of the rescued, not of poetic
expression of the soul purified by pity and terror, but of wild defiance of

27

inexorable Fate and undeniable Fact by an explosion of outrageous romantic lying?

What is the first demand of romance in a shipwreck? It is the cry of Women and Children first. No male creature is to step into a boat as long as there is a woman or child on the doomed ship. How the boat is to be navigated and rowed by babies and women occupied in holding the babies is not mentioned. The likelihood that no sensible woman would trust either herself or her child in a boat unless there was a considerable percentage of men on board is not considered. Women and Children first: that is the romantic formula. And never did the chorus of solemn delight at the strict observance of this formula by the British heroes on board the *Titanic* rise to sublimer strains than in the papers containing the first account of the wreck by a surviving eye-witness, Lady Duff Gordon. She described how she escaped in the captain's boat. There was one other woman in it, and ten men: twelve all told. One woman for every five men. Chorus: "Not once or twice in our rough island story," etc. etc.

Second romantic demand. Though all the men (except the foreigners, who must all be shot by stern British officers in attempting to rush the boats over the bodies of the women and children) must be heroes, the Captain must be a super-hero, a magnificent seaman, cool, brave, delighting in death and danger, and a living guarantee that the wreck was nobody's fault, but, on the contrary, a triumph of British navigation.

Such a man Captain Smith was enthusiastically proclaimed on the day when it was reported (and actually believed, apparently) that he had shot himself on the bridge, or shot the first officer, or been shot by the first officer, or shot anyhow to bring the curtain down effectively. Writers who had never heard of Captain Smith to that hour wrote of him as they would hardly write of Nelson. The one thing positively known was that Captain Smith had lost his ship by deliberately and knowingly steaming into an ice field at the highest speed he had coal for. He paid the penalty; so did most of those for whose lives he was responsible. Had he brought them and the ship safely to land, nobody would have taken the smallest notice of him.

Third romantic demand. The officers must be calm, proud, steady, unmoved in the intervals of shooting the terrified foreigners. The verdict that they had surpassed all expectations was unanimous. The actual evidence was that Mr. Ismay was told by the officer of his boat to go to hell, and that boats which were not full refused to go to the rescue of those who were struggling in the water in cork jackets. Reason frankly given: they were afraid. The fear was as natural as the officer's language to Mr. Ismay: who of us at home dare blame them or feel sure that we should have been any cooler or braver? But is it necessary to assure the world that only Englishmen could have behaved so heroically, and to compare their conduct with the hypothetic dastardliness which lascars or Italians or foreigners generally – say Nansen or Amundsen or the Duke of Abruzzi – would have shown in the same circumstances?

Fourth romantic demand. Everybody must face death without a tremor; and the band, according to the *Birkenhead* precedent, must play "Nearer, my God, to Thee" as an accompaniment to the invitation to Mr Ismay to go to hell. It was duly proclaimed that thus exactly it fell out. Actual evidence: the Captain and officers were so afraid of a panic that, though they knew the ship was sinking, they did not dare to tell the passengers so – especially the third-class passengers – and the band played Rag Times to reassure the passengers, who, therefore, did not get into the boats, and did not realise their situation until the boats were gone and the ship was standing on her head before plunging to the bottom.

I ask, What is the use of all this ghastly, blasphemous, inhuman, braggartly lying? Here is a calamity which might well make the proudest man humble, and the wildest joker serious. It makes us vainglorious, insolent and mendacious. At all events, that is what our journalists assumed. Were they right or wrong? Did the press really represent the public? I am afraid it did. Churchmen and statesmen took much the same tone. The effect on me was one of profound disgust, almost of national dishonour. Am I mad? Possibly. At all events, that is how I felt and how I feel about it. It seems to me that when deeply moved men should speak the truth. The English nation appears to take precisely the contrary view.

Commentary

One reason why this article has such force is because it is so tightly organised; each paragraph advances the argument, with the final sentence and its reference to 'The English nation' reminding the reader of the opening sentence and its reference to 'a modern nation'.

Having ended the first paragraph asking why there should be such 'romantic lying', Shaw structures the rest of the article around a series of four 'romantic demands'. These are:

1   the idea of women and children first is illogical, and men outnumbered women in the boats;
2   the captain was not a hero but an incompetent sailor who recklessly courted danger;

3   the officers were not calm and dignified, but frightened, as we should expect them to be, and

4   the band did not play a hymn, but a popular tune to hoodwink the passengers, especially the third-class ones, that everything was really all right.

Both the first and the last paragraphs contain a number of **rhetorical questions**. In the first paragraph he suggests what should be the mood, but is 'not'; in the last he points out what is 'wrong' and asserts the need for the 'truth'.

Another feature which gives the article its cohesion is the use of sarcasm. This is done in various ways. The reference to 'Chorus' in paragraph two, the description of the captain being shot in paragraph four, the comparison of the English with foreigners in paragraph five, are just a few examples of the mocking exaggeration which he sustains until the last sentence.

Although the article is full of wit and invention, it works because it is so clear and organised. Although for much of the time he is being ironic, there is never any doubt as to where he really stands. He does not just attack his opponents, he ridicules them, which is no doubt one of the reasons why Conan Doyle was so outraged.

Conclusion

This chapter has used one 'real' incident, the sinking of the *Titanic*, to investigate how authors use and shape material for different purposes.

Many of the ideas within the contextual framework in Chapter 1 have been explored, using the *Titanic* as a linking theme. With Hardy and Shaw in particular, we have seen how the writers' own values and assumptions have led them to challenge accepted views. We as contemporary readers are more likely to accept what they say than their contemporaries did; notions of heroism and nationalism are different now from those in 1912.

This means that while we are less shocked by their ideas, we may be surprised by what they leave out. With the Hardy poem in particular, we, as readers, have expectations that are not delivered. These expectations come from our previous knowledge of the subject, influenced in particular by recent films and by a renewed interest in the story.

Beryl Bainbridge, too, surprises us. In a much more modern view of the story, she does not look at the big picture, at causes and effects, but instead focuses on a much smaller scale, telling the story through the eyes of a minor player who does not fully realise what is going on. Again what we expect is not delivered, and this affects the ways in which we read the text.

Finally, all of the texts have distinctive linguistic features. As you would expect of a series of texts based on a real event, their own narrative organisation is vital to the way we read them. All of them have distinctive voices which help to shape the way we respond to them.

Chapter four

Attitudes, values and assumptions

Throughout this book it is stressed that analysing the contextual issues which surround texts involves recognising that when a text is read, the language user (or author) and the language receiver (or reader) are in a kind of relationship with each other.

Texts are produced by authors who live in the political and social world of their time, and we will gain a better understanding of their works by taking these contexts into account. It is equally true, though, that a text cannot have an existence independent of its readers. The readers recreate the text through bringing their own culturally-conditioned views and attitudes to bear on it; in other words, analysing a text includes looking at the attitudes, values and assumptions that we as readers find in it. These must be approached through an understanding of the political and social thought which shaped the author's ideas when the text was written, and the political and social thought which shape ours as we read. A useful word to use when referring to attitudes, values and assumptions is **ideology**, which is used to refer to the system of ideas characteristic of a group or of an individual.

It is sometimes our own ideology that we forget in this reading process. At least on a simple level, it is often quite easy to research some of the influences on an author but, in explaining how these influences affect the author's work, we often forget that our own ideology is making us read that work in a certain way. Different cultures, societies and individuals classify and understand the world in different ways. As readers we may like to think that we make choices about the way we view the world, that our views are somehow specific to us, but these choices are inevitably shaped for us by the society we live in.

Because texts mean different things to different readers at different times, it is crucial that readers on the one hand make critical judgements but, on the other, show that they understand different judgements to be possible. In other words, being a critical reader involves being aware that you have made choices from a range of options. This is why it is important to understand that texts contain meanings (plural) rather than a meaning (singular).

This unit will focus in particular on how texts can be read in terms of political ideology, looking especially at issues concerned with power and culture.

Analysing an advertisement

Although this book is primarily concerned with looking at literary texts, what may to some sound rather daunting terms – ideology, power, culture – can be introduced through first looking at an advert.

Task

The following advert for *Nurofen Advance* first appeared in British newspapers in 1998.

Read the advert carefully and then note down answers to the following questions; a commentary follows, but refer to it only when you have completed your own responses.

1   Do you know what metaphor is suggested by the visual image? If the answer is yes, how do you know? Who might not know what is suggested?
2   Adverts often suggest that the product being sold is in some way special. What is special about *Nurofen Advance*? Find all the linguistic references which back up this idea.
3   Can you say how these linguistic references connect with the answer to question 1? Can you find any phrases which have two potential meanings?

Text   *Nurofen* **advertisement**

NEW NUROFEN ADVANCE.
FAST ROUTE
TO PAIN RELIEF.

When you haven't got time for pain, try new Nurofen Advance. Nurofen Advance is different because it contains a unique ingredient. This is specially developed to be rapidly absorbed and get to the site of pain. Fast.

CONTAINS IBUPROFEN LYSINE

NUROFEN ADVANCE. FAST RELIEF FOR PAIN.

Available from your pharmacist. Always read the label.

4   A created reader – 'you' – is referred to in this advert. What sort of life-style is created for this reader? What is said that will make the product sound impressive to this created reader?

5   Weighing up all the evidence you have collected in answering the above questions, and taking into account anything else you have noticed, can you work out an ideological position that is being taken? In other words, does this advert have a view of modern life in Britain that it is assuming the reader will agree with?

Commentary

The visual image suggests a sign of a British motorway with a turning off it. The motorway, the fast road ahead, is linked to *Nurofen Advance*. If you want to make fast progress, this is the route to take. Most British readers will have recognised this sign – both a sign literally, but also a sign that metaphorically signifies something – because they have travelled on motorways and so have experienced seeing such signs before. Overseas readers may be less familiar with British road signs. If they have similar signs in their culture, then they could probably work out what it signifies. If they have no such roads or signs in their culture, the reference would be more puzzling.

In terms of the language used, there is a whole network of references to moving forward at speed. These include:

advance
fast route
haven't got time
rapidly
fast
rapid
get to the site of

These words all refer back to the visual sign, and its suggestion of getting somewhere fast. 'When you haven't got time for pain' will be recognised by many readers as having two meanings. It works within the idea of moving fast, but it also has the idiomatic sense of not liking something, wanting to get rid of it. Another phrase with two meanings is 'get to the site of'. To get to the site of something is to end your journey. But in terms of pain-relief, it means that *Nurofen* gets to the centre of the pain, and cures it.

So far then, through the use of signs and verbal metaphors, a story has been constructed which readers within British culture are likely to understand. In this story there is also a 'you', a constructed reader or narratee for whom the text is apparently written. As we discussed in Chapter 2, just as it can be a mistake to think that the narrator of a story or poem is the author, so it can be a mistake to suppose that the narratee, the reader to whom the narrative is addressed, is also the real reader. In this case the narratee is a person with certain attitudes. They have no time for pain, they want things to happen fast – in the implied language of this advert, they live life in the fast lane. They also seek new ways of dealing with things; the word 'New' is highlighted and the product is 'different' because it contains a 'unique ingredient'.

The real reader, then, is faced with a certain view of life and how it should be. Pain should be conquered fast, life should be got on with, there should be no hold-ups or delays. This view contains an ideological perspective. The real reader, it is hoped, will be keen to take a mild drug to eliminate pain, pain which may well have been caused by the pace of life in the first place. Attitudes are called ideological, though, when it is possible to conceive that there could be another way of looking at things. In some cultures, in parts of the world other than Britain, pain is not treated with drugs, success is not measured by speed of action; readers from those cultures would be much more uncertain of what the advert means and how to understand it.

It should be equally clear that this advert belongs not only to a certain place but to a certain time, the late twentieth century. In its representation of ideas and its ideology, this advert could not have been written in the previous century. It could, of course, be read in the future, but it will be seen differently, its meaning is not fixed. Consider your response when you come across old adverts; their representation of attitudes, although perhaps only forty or so years old, often seem very different from those you hold now.

This analysis of an advert shows three things:

1   most texts contain cultural attitudes or ideologies;
2   how texts are read depends on the reader's ideology;
3   apparently simple texts like this are in fact often very good examples of ideology at work. It is not just literature which holds cultural significance.

It should also be clear that in analysing this advert we have applied all five parts of the context frame established in Chapter 1. Although this text is anonymously written, it belongs to the culture of its time. The reader's cultural baggage has also been examined. The text will in due course have its own history. We used linguistic analysis to see how the text works and this in turn led to analysis of possible readings.

Task

To gain another perspective on what has been learnt so far in this unit, now attempt to write your own advert.

1   Decide on a product; ideally this should be one which will carry strong cultural overtones; such as a car, a cosmetic, an alcoholic drink. Name your invented product and write a piece of advertising copy for it. Give a broad outline of the visual images which will accompany your written text. Consider also the publication in which it will appear.
2   When you have done the above, swap adverts with a partner or partners. Now become a reader of their text, while they read yours. Provide the writer of the text with an analysis which shows what ideological positions they have taken according to your reading of their text. Then see if they agree.

Jane Austen   *Sense and Sensibility*

It is now time to look at attitudes, values and assumptions as they appear in literary texts. Jane Austen's *Sense and Sensibility* was first published in 1811. If modern readers have any preconceptions about Jane Austen, they are likely to be influenced by her reputation as a novelist who writes about a very small section of society, a section to which she herself belonged. Television and film adaptations of her novels are numerous, and have been hugely popular. They present a very photogenic picture of English estates and glamorous couples; there are no major events as such, but much emphasis on heterosexual relationships where, providing the characters are morally good, love wins out in the end. It would seem that a Jane Austen novel is one text where the attitudes and values belong to ideas of personal relationships leading to marriage rather than anything to do with power, culture and politics.

To put this hypothesis to the test, you are going to work on the opening of Jane Austen's *Sense and Sensibility*. Openings of novels are often worth looking at because they are, by necessity, to do with **establishment**. This means that the characters are introduced and settings are geographically and socially located. In addition to these spatial aspects, establishment is also often concerned with aspects of time, such as when the action is taking place and what has gone before. Openings therefore contain important material, which the author will have carefully placed. Read the extract printed below a couple of times, and try to get a general sense of what is going on. To help you understand what is a rather complex set of circumstances, here is a summary:

> Norland Park in Sussex is the home of the Dashwood family. Before the action of this story starts, an unnamed single male member of the family lived there with his sister. She died, so he invited his nephew Henry Dashwood and his family to live with him. Henry has one son by his first marriage and three daughters from his second.
>
> The old man dies and the inheritance passes to Henry Dashwood and then to his son, who is already wealthy through (a) what his mother left him and (b) his wife's dowry. This leaves Henry's wife and three daughters short of income, should Henry die – which he does soon after.

Text   *Sense and Sensibility*

The family of Dashwood had long been settled in Sussex. Their estate was large, and their residence was at Norland Park, in the centre of their property, where for many generations they had lived in so respectable a manner as to engage the general good opinion of their surrounding acquaintance. The late owner of this estate was a single man, who lived to a very advanced age, and who for many years of his life had a constant companion and housekeeper in his sister. But her death, which happened ten years before his own, produced a great alteration in his home; for to supply her loss, he invited and received into his house the family of his nephew, Mr. Henry Dashwood, the legal inheritor of the Norland estate, and the person to whom he intended to bequeath it. In the society of his nephew and niece, and their children, the old gentleman's days were comfortably spent. His attachment to them all increased. The constant attention of Mr. and Mrs. Henry Dashwood to his wishes, which proceeded not merely from interest, but from goodness of heart, gave him every degree of solid comfort which his age could receive; and the cheerfulness of the children added a relish to his existence.

By a former marriage, Mr. Henry Dashwood had one son; by his present lady, three daughters. The son, a steady, respectable young man, was amply provided for by the fortune of his mother, which had been large, and half of which devolved on him on his coming of age. By his own marriage, likewise, which happened soon afterwards, he added to his wealth. To him, therefore, the succession to the Norland estate was not so really important as to his sisters; for their fortune, independent of what might arise to them from their father's inheriting that property, could be but small. Their mother had nothing, and their father only seven thousand pounds in his own disposal; for the remaining moiety of his first wife's fortune was also secured to her child, and he had only a life-interest in it.

The old gentleman died; his will was read, and like almost every other will, gave as much disappointment as pleasure. He was neither so unjust, nor so ungrateful, as to leave his estate from his nephew; but he left it to him on such terms as destroyed half the value of the bequest. Mr. Dashwood had wished for it more for the sake of his wife and daughters than for himself or his son; but to his son, and his son's son, a child of four years old, it was secured, in such a way, as to leave to himself no power of providing for those who were most dear to him, and who most needed a provision, by any charge on the estate, or by any sale of its valuable woods. The whole was tied up for the benefit of this child, who, in occasional visits with his father and mother at Norland had so far gained on the affections of his uncle, by such attractions as are by no means unusual in children of two or three years old: an imperfect articulation, an earnest desire of having his own way, many cunning tricks, and a great deal of noise, as to outweigh all the value of all the attention which, for years, he had received from his niece and her daughters. He meant not to be unkind, however, and, as a mark of his affection for the three girls, he left them a thousand pounds a-piece.

Mr. Dashwood's disappointment was at first severe; but his temper was cheerful and sanguine, and he might reasonably hope to live many years, and by living economically, lay by a considerable sum from the produce of an estate already large, and capable of almost immediate improvement. But the fortune, which had been so tardy in coming, was his only one twelvemonth. He survived his uncle no longer; and ten thousand pounds, including the late legacies, was all that remained for his widow and daughters.

It may be that you found this quite difficult to follow, even with the summary. This is difficult to follow because of what it is about – legal inheritance. You are now going to search for words and phrases which belong in **semantic fields**; in other words they are in the same area of meaning. In doing this you will begin to identify some of the areas that the text itself highlights.

Task

Find as many words/phrases as you can for the following areas:

◎   property and money
◎   family
◎   male power and authority
◎   behaviour and manners
◎   love and friendship
◎   work

Once you have done this research, try to come up with some ideas about the attitudes and values which underpin this extract. If possible, compare your ideas with others in a group, and then the whole class. Once you have done this, consider the following:

1   What are the attitudes and values which can be found in this extract? How do you as a reader respond to them?
2   Does Jane Austen ask the reader to question these attitudes and values or does she seem to expect the reader to accept them?

When you have completed these tasks, compare your answers with the commentary which follows.

Commentary

The novel opens with names of a family and their estate in Sussex, in the south of England. The family has lived at Norland Park for a long time, and so has real claim to ownership of the property. Much of the extract is about inheritance and wealth, with the two closely linked; although who gets what is a matter of concern, there is no doubt that the property will be passed on within the family.

Family relationships are given in detail; nephews, sons, nieces, daughters, sisters, fathers, mothers, uncles are all mentioned. It is the

41

males, however, who hold power. The old man has a companion in his sister who is also his housekeeper; once she dies she is replaced by a nephew and his family who stand to gain once he has died. Henry Dashwood's son has wealth and therefore power, even though his original money has come from two different women. When the will is read it goes to three generations of males, leaving the women relatively little, at least in proportion to what is available. (In fact ten thousand pounds would have been a large sum to many in those days.)

A number of words are used to describe behaviour and responses: 'respectable'; 'good opinion'; 'comfortably spent'; 'solid comfort'; 'steady, respectable'; '(not) unjust or ungrateful'; 'cheerful and sanguine'. The dominant ideas are of comfort, respectability and decency towards others, although how others are treated is often reported in double negatives; 'not ungrateful' does not carry the full weight of 'grateful'. This is the case when the old man's provision for the girls is mentioned. 'He meant not to be unkind, however, and as a mark of his affection for the three girls, he left them a thousand pounds each'. This may be ironic, but for a modern reader it is hard to tell; what was the value of a thousand pounds in those days? If Jane Austen is indeed saying that his treatment of the girls is not fair, it comes across in an understated way.

Words like 'acquaintance', 'companion', 'attachment', 'attention', are used to describe intimacy between people. Despite the fact that there are close family ties, there is little suggestion of strong emotion. Mr and Mrs Henry Dashwood attend to the old man's wishes 'not merely from interest, but from goodness of heart'. It is their self-interest which is mentioned first, apparently without any irony. The fact that they hope to gain from being with the old man is accepted and expected.

What we have seen so far is a detailed picture of social power and values. How you respond to it, of course, depends in part upon how you interpret this picture. One view would be that it is an horrendously repressive, narrow and emotionally-crippling world that is presented to us, where, by accidents of birth and the power of legacy, men control a world of property and family which at best offers them sycophantic respect. In taking this view you would be, quite justifiably, using modern values by which to judge an earlier age.

A different view would be one which attempts to look at the picture as an historic representation of social values as they existed then, like it or not. This view would focus on Jane Austen's detailed depiction of a world she knew well, a world which she, as a woman, was in no position to challenge. Her skill at questioning some of the motives of those involved would be highlighted, rather than her failure to question the values of a conservative property-based élite to which she herself tenuously belonged.

The final semantic field you were asked to search for was a bit of a trick, in that in the sense we would know it, there is no mention of paid work at all. Admittedly the old man's sister is a housekeeper, presumably unpaid, and the relatives all arrive to be a companion for the old man – but only with the promise of an inheritance to come. Above all, in an extract where money is crucial, where actual sums of money are mentioned and large ones at that, there is no mention where the money has come from, or how it is invested within a capitalist system.

From our historical knowledge of the time, we can speculate how people like the Dashwoods did make money: the estate would be farmed by tenants who would pay rents; money would be invested in colonies abroad; investments would quite possibly be made in slave-trading enterprises. But Jane Austen does not seem interested in how the money was made, just how it will be passed on. Is this because she did not know about such matters? Is it because she assumed her readers would not need to be told as they knew already? Is it because it was bad manners in polite circles to talk about how capitalism actually worked? None of these questions can be answered definitely, because Jane Austen is silent about them, but in asking the questions, we are following what for us are valid lines of enquiry.

The important theoretical point to make here is about **absence**. We, as readers, often become so involved in what **is** in a text that we overlook what is not. The attitudes and values in a text can sometimes be seen by what is not in a text as well as by what is. Jane Austen is known for the subtle irony of her writing, and there are moments in this extract where it is possible that Jane Austen is being ironic, especially when she describes the apportionment of the will; but her failure to mention where the money comes from, how it grows, what work it is doing in the big wide world, suggests that if she has doubts about anything, it is not about the structures of early nineteenth-century capitalism. There does not appear to be any irony in her view of the system by which money is gained and passed on to others. Some readers and critics would argue that Jane Austen should not be criticised for her acceptance of the social and economic values of her time; she was, after all, of her own time. But we are also of our time, and, as readers, we are bound from our own cultural perspective to question what she takes for granted. Interpreting Jane Austen, and indeed any writer, depends on (a) who does the interpreting; (b) when the interpretation is done and (c) where interpreters come from in terms of their own values and beliefs.

What Jane Austen has done in this opening section is establish the background for her plot, which will follow the fortunes of the three women disadvantaged by a bad will. She has also shown that although she will question some of the actions of those within a strict political and social system, she will not question the system itself.

Throughout the discussion of *Sense and Sensibility* above, it has been assumed that the narrative voice is very close to Jane Austen herself, and so quite distant from the story she is telling. If you re-read the first paragraph, you get an immediate sense that the narrator knows everything – events, characters and their characteristics, motives for action. This form of narrative, typical of many nineteenth-century novels, is known as the **omniscient** voice; omniscient because the narrator knows everything and is in total control. Although we cannot assume that the narrative voice belongs to Jane Austen herself, we can nonetheless safely presume that it voices values she herself held.

The approach to analysing both the *Nurofen* advert and the opening of *Sense and Sensibility* involved looking at language – at semantic fields in particular – to highlight areas of the texts worth focusing on. Linguistic analysis is of great value when analysing text, provided it is used as a tool to explore the ideas and values which the text contains; it is of much less value if it becomes an end in itself. Finding vocabulary which belongs to the same semantic field is of limited value unless you go on to say what this choice of vocabulary tells you about the meanings that are created within the text.

Mark Twain *Huckleberry Finn*

A very different sort of narrative voice from *Sense and Sensibility* can be seen in the opening of *Huckleberry Finn* by Mark Twain. Through an exploration of this opening, we shall see (a) whether it is possible to detect the author's values and assumptions underlying a text when it is narrated in the first person by a character in the story, and (b) whether a first person narrative allows the author to challenge, rather than support, the orthodox social values of the time.

Task

The following forms the first part of the opening chapter of *Huckleberry Finn*. It was first published in 1884, eight years after the success of *Tom Sawyer*. First read the extract and then re-read it, this time making notes on the following questions:

1   How is this unusual as the start of a novel?
2   Make two lists, one for the attitudes and values shown by Widow Douglas/Miss Watson, and one for the attitudes and values of Huck Finn.

When you have done this, work at the following questions, making sure that you re-read parts of the text as necessary.

3   Review the lists you have made; write a paragraph which sums up the values of Widow Douglas/Miss Watson and then one which sums up the values of Huck Finn.
4   Look closely at the second paragraph, up to 'she would civilize me'. What are the Widow's motives for taking in Huck Finn? Why doesn't Huck see this?
5   Of the two contrasting sets of values that you have been exploring, which do you think Twain intends the reader to prefer? How does he shape our reading to make us do so?
6   Finally, to complete this exercise, and to link it with some earlier work in this chapter on types of narrative, re-write paragraphs two and three as though the novel were written with a distant third-person narrative, as was the case with *Sense and Sensibility*. What have you found in doing this?

When you have completed these tasks, read the commentary which follows the text.

Text   *Huckleberry Finn*

You don't know about me, without you have read a book by the name of *The Adventures of Tom Sawyer*, but that ain't no matter. That book was made by Mr Mark Twain, and he told the truth, mainly. There was things which he stretched, but mainly he told the truth. That is nothing. I never seen anybody but lied, one time or another, without it was Aunt Polly, or the widow, or maybe Mary. Aunt Polly – Tom's Aunt Polly, she is – and

Mary, and the Widow Douglas, is all told about in that book – which is mostly a true book; with some stretchers, as I said before.

Now the way that the book winds up, is this: Tom and me found the money that the robbers hid in the cave, and it made us rich. We got six thousand dollars apiece – all gold. It was an awful sight of money when it was piled up. Well, Judge Thatcher, he took it and put it out at interest, and it fetched us a dollar a day apiece, all the year round – more than a body could tell what to do with. The Widow Douglas, she took me for her son, and allowed she would civilize me; but it was rough living in the house all the time, considering how dismal regular and decent the widow was in all her ways; and so when I couldn't stand it no longer, I lit out. I got into my old rags and my sugar-hogshead* again, and was free and satisfied. But Tom Sawyer he hunted me up and said he was going to start a band of robbers, and I might join if I would go back to the widow and be respectable. So I went back.

The widow she cried over me, and called me a poor lost lamb, and she called me a lot of other names, too, but she never meant no harm by it. She put me in them new clothes again, and I couldn't do nothing but sweat and sweat, and feel all cramped up. Well, then, the old thing commenced again. The widow rung a bell for supper, and you had to come to time. When you got to the table you couldn't go right to eating, but you had to wait for the widow to tuck down her head and grumble a little over the victuals, though there warn't really anything the matter with them. That is, nothing only everything was cooked by itself. In a barrel of odds and ends it is different; things get mixed up, and the juice kind of swaps around, and the things go better.

After supper she got out her book and learned me about Moses and the 'Bulrushers'; and I was in a sweat to find out all about him; but by and by she let it out that Moses had been dead a considerable long time; so then I didn't care no more about him; because I don't take no stock in dead people.

Pretty soon I wanted to smoke, and asked the widow to let me. But she wouldn't. She said it was a mean practice and wasn't clean, and I must try to not do it any more. That is just the way with some people. They get down on a thing when they don't know nothing about it. Here she was a-bothering about Moses, which was no kin to her, and no use to anybody, being gone, you see, yet finding a power of fault with me for doing a thing that had some good in it. And she took snuff too; of course that was all right, because she done it herself.

* *hogshead*: A large barrel.

46

Her sister, Miss Watson, a tolerable slim old maid, with goggles on, had just come to live with her, and took a set at me now, with a spelling book. She worked me middling hard for about an hour, and then the widow made her ease up. I couldn't stood it much longer. Then for an hour it was deadly dull, and I was fidgety. Miss Watson would say, 'Don't put your feet up there, Huckleberry'; and 'Don't scrunch up like that, Huckleberry – set up straight'; and pretty soon she would say, 'Don't gap and stretch like that, Huckleberry – why don't you try to behave?' Then she told me all about the bad place, and I said I wished I was there. She got mad, then, but I didn't mean no harm. All I wanted was to go somewheres; all I wanted was a change, I warn't particular. She said it was wicked to say what I said; said she wouldn't say it for the whole world; *she* was going to live so as to go to the good place. Well, I couldn't see no advantage in going where she was going, so I made up my mind I wouldn't try for it. But I never said so, because it would only make trouble, and wouldn't do no good.

Commentary

The opening paragraph of the novel is unusual for a number of reasons:

1   It sounds as if the narrator/character is talking directly to us.
2   It makes it quite clear that this is a sequel to a previous novel.
3   But this idea of the sequel is spoken by a character *within* the story ...
4   ... who then goes on to mention the author.

What we expect from a novel is challenged. We expect the novel will present itself to us as though 'real', but what Twain does here is make it very clear that we are reading a novel; that truth and reality are relative.

The statement by Huck that everyone has lied at some time, including the author, is an important part of how Twain establishes the character of his narrator. Huck Finn is both perceptive and naïve – he can see through hypocrisy in one sense, yet fails to see, perhaps because he is shown to be optimistic about the motives of others, the true extent of the Widow's self-interest. A key word in the second paragraph is the word 'civilize' – what in the Widow's terms does this mean?

Your lists for 2 in the above task may have included some of the following:

1   Attitudes and Values of Widow Douglas/Miss Watson: belief in outward appearance; bound by time and convention; narrowly religious with threats of hell; hypocritical about smoking; bound by routine.
2   Attitudes and Values of Huck Finn: wants freedom from social rules; has no interest in money; dislikes the conventions of civilised living; wants to live in the here and now; wants experience to be interesting, likes 'mixed up' food; doesn't want to upset others.

The above can quite clearly be seen through what Huck's narrative tells us, although he does not always put it in such analytical terms; after all, Twain is at great pains to show that his responses are natural rather than schooled. One thing he does not comment on at all, but which Twain leaves for the reader to pick up, is the real motive for the Widow to want Huck as her son. By following the fact that Huck is rich with the sentence 'The Widow Douglas, she took me for her son', Twain makes it evident to the reader that the Widow's motives are mercenary, she wants the money. Behind the Christian façade of good works lies greed. The sequence of the sentences, the shape of the paragraph, make this clear. Huck, though, because he has no such interest nor motives himself, fails to comment on this, or to notice it.

Twain, then, intends the reader to be on the side of Huck. How readers interpret Twain's creation of Huck depends to some extent on their own starting-point. Some critics, for example, have seen Huck as an embodiment of American free spirit, of a doomed attempt to break away from essentially European values. Others have seen him as representing pure moral values in the face of organised religion and its hypocrisy. If you read the whole novel, you will find other value systems are explored, especially ideas surrounding slavery through the character of the runaway Jim.

Students who attempted question 6, above, found that re-writing paragraphs 2 and 3 in a distant third-person voice created a very different effect. Not only did the narrative become very flat, making Huck seem rather featureless, but they also found it harder to see the attitudes and values of the characters coming through. This emphasises that narrative, and the choices that an author makes from those that are available, contribute significantly to the way ideology is seen to work in texts. Whether it is a distant omniscient narrative, or a naïve first-person narrative, to name the two seen in this chapter, the narrative method is part of the process whereby ideas and ideologies are communicated.

In other words, attitudes and values that can be found in texts do not exist independently of the other things at work, such as language, narrative, structure. Meanings are woven into the very fabric of the text – the word 'text' itself belonging to the family of words which includes textile.

Daniel Defoe   *Robinson Crusoe*

This chapter will conclude by looking at an extract from *Robinson Crusoe* by Daniel Defoe. The novel was published in 1719. Although it is not widely read these days, it is one of those books which most people have heard of. It has a cultural existence beyond its readership. A common notice found in many workplaces goes something like: 'The only person to get everything done by Friday was Robinson Crusoe.' Most people know that Friday was some sort of worker and Robinson Crusoe some sort of boss. Looking at the point at which they first meet helps us to understand how ideology in texts can be discovered.

Task

At the point where this extract begins, Crusoe has been marooned for many years on the island. Then, for the first time, he meets Friday. Read the extract and answer the following question:

> What assumptions and values about power and control are contained in the way Robinson Crusoe describes his first meeting with Friday? How do you respond to these assumptions and values?

Think in particular about the assumptions that Crusoe makes about Friday, and your attitudes to these assumptions.

49

Text *Robinson Crusoe*

I Call Him Friday

He was a comely, handsome fellow, perfectly well made, with straight strong limbs, not too large, tall and well-shaped, and, as I reckon, about twenty-six years of age. He had a very good countenance, not a fierce and surly aspect, but seemed to have something very manly in his face, and yet he had all the sweetness and softness of an European in his countenance too, especially when he smiled. His hair was long and black, not curled like wool; his forehead very high and large; and a great vivacity and sparkling sharpness in his eyes. The colour of his skin was not quite black, but very tawny; and yet not of an ugly yellow, nauseous tawny, as the Brazilians, and Virginians, and other natives of America are; but of a bright kind of a dun olive colour that had in it something very agreeable, though not very easy to describe. His face was round and plump; his nose small, not flat like the Negroes', a very good mouth, thin lips, and his fine teeth well set, and white as ivory. After he had slumbered, rather than slept, about half an hour, he waked again, and comes out of the cave to me, for I had been milking my goats, which I had in the enclosure just by. When he espied me, he came running to me, laying himself down again upon the ground, with all the possible signs of an humble, thankful disposition, making many antic gestures to show it. At last he lays his head flat upon the ground, close to my foot, and sets my other foot upon his head, as he had done before; and after this, made all the signs to me of subjection, servitude, and submission imaginable, to let me know how he would serve me as long as he lived; I understood him in many things and let him know I was very well pleased with him; in a little time I began to speak to him and teach him to speak to me; and first, I made him know his name should be Friday, which was the day I saved his life; I called him so for the memory of the time; I likewise taught him to say "Master," and then let him know that was to be my name; I likewise taught him to say "yes" and "no" and to know the meaning of them; I gave him some milk in an earthen pot and let him see me drink it before him and sop my bread in it; and I gave him a cake of bread to do the like, which he quickly complied with, and made signs that it was very good for him.

Commentary

This is a first person narrative, so we cannot automatically assume that what the character believes in is what the author believes in too. If we were meant to question Crusoe's views, though, we would expect the author to make it sound ironic, to give us some sort of clue that we shouldn't take it seriously. There certainly don't seem to be any such clues here, so if we make a list of Crusoe's attitudes, we can say that they are pretty much Defoe's too.

Crusoe's attitudes

1   He observes Friday's appearance as though he is some sort of working animal, a horse maybe.
2   He makes value judgements based on skin and hair characteristics, believing European to be best.
3   He accepts without question that Friday sees him as a superior, and that he is indeed superior.
4   In naming Friday he (a) assumes he has no name already; (b) gives him a name in English; (c) gives him a name that is not a standard name, merely a day of the week. So although Crusoe gives the name, it is one which makes sure that Friday is not to be considered as 'normal'.
5   The first words he teaches Friday are about servitude and obedience. Crusoe does not want to talk with Friday, merely to command him.

The modern readers' attitudes

While we can understand why Crusoe has the attitudes listed above – they were the predominant attitudes held at the time in a country beginning to expand into a colonial power – this does not mean that we at the present day will readily accept them: there is a tension between what we see as an ideology belonging to a certain time, and the ideological views which we ourselves hold.

Read the following extracts taken from the work of some students. Compare your ideas with theirs. To what extent have you agreed with what they say? Or disagreed? Or noticed different things?

1   The overall value that seems to be contained in the way that Crusoe describes his first meeting with Friday is one of racial

superiority by Crusoe. There is evidence in the title of the chapter 'I call him Friday'. This suggests that Friday has no say in this, that Crusoe has given him this name and that is final.

The fact that Crusoe only trains Friday to say 'master', 'yes' and 'no' shows the amount of control he has over Friday. Friday can only do what Crusoe tells him. His limited vocabulary prevents him from arguing. By limiting his vocabulary he is reducing Friday's power and giving it to himself.

2 Daniel Defoe wrote *Robinson Crusoe* at a time when racism wasn't even regarded as an issue. That doesn't mean though that I as a modern reader cannot find much of this section offensive. In Defoe's time slavery was a major trade and the white middle class who would have read this book would probably have had connections with slavery.

The idea of the black man being very much a second-rate human is evident throughout this text. Crusoe thinks he is 'the dominant breed', whereas Friday shows signs of 'subjection, servitude and submission'. The fact that the text does not contain a hint of irony and is expressed as being the natural course of how a first meeting should be will be very problematic for a modern reader.

3 Although the narrator, Crusoe, begins by complimenting Friday, he only admires his physical appearance. The way in which he describes Friday's build and teeth is more like the description of an animal than a man.

When Friday volunteers to be Crusoe's servant, the white man doesn't express any surprise or wonder why. Even though they are the only two men on the desert island, Crusoe automatically becomes the master, because he is white and European.

4 I find it interesting that Friday seems to have no objection to what is going on, and feels that things are as they should be. This could be because it is Crusoe who is telling the story, who is so sure he is right, he wouldn't recognise anything else. But it also seems as though Defoe accepts it all too, especially the bit when Friday sees Crusoe and immediately falls at his feet.

A central idea in this chapter has been that different cultures, societies and individuals view the world in different ways. How has your understanding of this idea been developed by your responses to

Robinson Crusoe and a comparison of your answers with those of these students?

Conclusion

This chapter has looked at the way attitudes and values can be found in texts, and how readers bring their own attitudes and values to their readings of texts. By using an advert as an example, we saw how texts can contain an ideological perspective which says something about the culture from which they originate. Whether we accept this ideological perspective, either consciously or unconsciously, depends in part upon our own ideological standpoint.

Two texts, Jane Austen's *Sense and Sensibility* and Daniel Defoe's *Robinson Crusoe*, were explored from a **post-colonial** perspective. In other words, they were written at a time when attitudes to colonial expansion and exploitation were very different from those of today. While understanding that they were written at different times, this does not mean that we do not use our own knowledge of colonialism when we read the texts today.

In the case of *Sense and Sensibility*, we noticed that our interpretation was affected by what was absent in the text, what it did **not** say about money and where it comes from. With *Robinson Crusoe,* we saw how the first person narrative, the sheer confidence that Crusoe has in his assumptions, shaped our responses as modern readers.

The narrative method of the *Huckleberry Finn* extract was also an important factor in our perception of attitudes and values. This is the opening of the novel: establishing characterisation, and our interpretations of it, was crucial. We saw not only a first person narrator, but one whose naïveté made the reader see beyond the stated to something more profound. Different characters had been established, it seemed, to represent different ideological perspectives.

Chapter five

Finding meanings in poetry

In the previous chapter we explored some of the ways in which attitudes and values can be found in prose texts. In this chapter the topic will be explored further, with a particular focus on ambiguity in texts. The Latin prefix 'ambi' means 'both ways' – so a person who is ambidextrous can write with both hands. In a literary sense, though, the word ambiguity is used to describe an unlimited number of possible meanings in a text. This ambiguity is not a sin – as it might be if you were drawing up a legal document for instance – but a positive and necessary virtue of texts which are re-interpreted each time they are read.

Although many of the ideas and critical vocabulary that were used in the last chapter will also be used here, they will be applied to the genre of poetry.

Philip Larkin   *Mr Bleaney*

Unlike novels, most poems are relatively brief and can be read quickly – they can also be re-read. These readings can be both private and public. Reading a poem silently creates a different impact than reading it aloud, while hearing it read aloud by someone else is different again. Hearing the poem read to you alone is different from hearing it read to a group, where you may well be influenced by the reactions of others. Although it is possible to buy tapes of novels read aloud, most of us read them silently to ourselves, and we rarely read them in one sitting. Although we may occasionally re-read a novel – because it is a favourite or because we are studying it for exams – usually we read a novel only once.

The first poem to be explored is *Mr Bleaney* by Philip Larkin. It was first published in 1955. You will be given a range of tasks on this poem, each task followed by a short commentary.

Task

Read the poem and jot down any ideas that occur to you on a first reading. Note down any parts of the poem you find difficult or puzzling.

Text   *Mr Bleaney*

'This was Mr Bleaney's room. He stayed
The whole time he was at the Bodies, till
They moved him.' Flowered curtains, thin and frayed,
Fall to within five inches of the sill,

Whose window shows a strip of building land,
Tussocky, littered. 'Mr Bleaney took
My bit of garden properly in hand.'
Bed, upright chair, sixty-watt bulb, no hook

Behind the door, no room for books or bags –
'I'll take it.' So it happens that I lie
Where Mr Bleaney lay, and stub my fags
On the same saucer-souvenir, and try

Stuffing my ears with cotton-wool, to drown
The jabbering set he egged her on to buy.
I know his habits – what time he came down,
His preference for sauce to gravy, why

He kept on plugging at the four aways –
Likewise their yearly frame: the Frinton folk
Who put him up for summer holidays,
And Christmas at his sister's house in Stoke.

But if he stood and watched the frigid wind
Tousling the clouds, lay on the fusty bed
Telling himself that this was home, and grinned,
And shivered, without shaking off the dread

That how we live measures our own nature,
And at his age having no more to show
Than one hired box should make him pretty sure
He warranted no better, I don't know.

Now look at the title. It consists of a name, but given that this is a fictional name, and that Larkin could have chosen any name, the fact that he chose this one must be significant.

Fictional names carry **connotations**; in other words they create an association for the reader. These connotations do not, on first reading, have anything to do with knowing the character, as they might if the name belonged to a famous actual person whose existence was well known. Instead, these connotations come from other sources. Write down the name 'Mr Bleaney' in the centre of a page and then in spidergram-form, jot down any connotations that come from the name, and say why.

Commentary

A group of students working at this task came up with the following:

'formal'	*Mr* Bleaney rather than a first name.
'dull'	by association with other words beginning with the letters 'bl', i.e. blank, bleary, blind, blanket, blotchy, bland, bleak, bleach, blur, blunt.
'ordinary'/ 'undistinguished'	long sound of 'ea' with 'y' at the end. Not exotic, unusual, double-barrelled etc.

By looking at the name alone, the group worked out that the title was sending out an advance signal about this fictional man. It would come as a major surprise if this character turned out to be an heroic figure. Through prior knowledge about language and connotations they had already begun to think about the poem.

Task

The title leads the reader to believe that this is going to be a poem centred on a fictional character. He is not, though, the only person in the poem. Write down other people mentioned in the poem. Then try to work out which of the cast of characters is ultimately given the most significance by Larkin. Note down your reasons.

Commentary

In addition to Mr Bleaney, there is the unnamed 'her', presumably the landlady who rents out the room; there is the 'I' who narrates the poem; and there is 'we', an unspecific group hard to pin down at this stage.

Because you may already have a sense that the poem is bleak, and you may know that Larkin has a reputation as a pessimist, you may be tempted to think that the 'I' of the poem is Larkin himself. This is not necessarily the case; after all, we do not presume that the first person narrator of a novel is the author. For this reason we need to use the term **persona** to describe the narrative 'I'. Of the cast-list, it is unlikely that you will have chosen the landlady as the most significant. From the other three, though, it becomes more difficult. Mr Bleaney has the title, yet is never seen in present time and is only ever spoken about – his actual words are not recorded.

Just as a title is an important part of a poem, so is the conclusion. The final person to be mentioned is 'I', it is the persona who has the last word. But it is hardly a strong last word, because it is all about doubt. Does this mean that it is 'we' who are the most important, because after all the 'we' also includes the persona? It is not an easy question to answer.

Task

Make notes on the following and how you respond to them:

◎   Mr Bleaney's life and habits;
◎   the room and its surrounds;
◎   the life-style of the persona/narrator.

Commentary

Mr Bleaney's fictional life is signalled by habits, objects and places. He worked at the *Bodies*, an unexplained reference, but one which sounds impersonal, disembodied. To understand fully what his habits represent, you need some knowledge of how they would have been viewed in the 1950s, when the poem was written. In addition to gardening and listening with the landlady to the radio which 'jabbers', he preferred sauce to gravy – unexciting meals. He kept on plugging at the four aways, a minor form of gambling, with low stakes and low winnings, on the football pools; he went on holidays to the unglamorous resort of Frinton; he visited his sister, rather than a girlfriend, at the equally unglamorous Stoke. As we suspected from the first task, this is a very dull man; yet the landlady admires him and clearly sees him as superior to her new guest or so the new guest thinks. The room too is very dowdy. It has an ugly view, no lampshade, a dull bulb in the light, frayed curtains which are too short, a saucer as an ashtray.

The persona, meanwhile, is both different and the same. He has books and he does his best to ignore the landlady. Yet he spends his time doing nothing more than smoking. His life too has little going for it. Unlike Mr Bleaney, he goes nowhere.

Task

The next task is a little harder. Although the poem has a regular rhyme scheme and a regular verse form, its **syntax** – or sentence structure – is more fluid, moving across lines and verses. The first sentence is short, simple and emphatic. Others, which provide much of the detail, are longer, although not complex in their structure. The last sentence, where we are looking for the poem's final take on the ideas it has so far presented, begins at the start of the penultimate verse and continues, via a series of **clauses**, through to the end. (A clause is a structural unit which is part of a sentence.)

1   Make a list of the component parts of this final sentence.
2   Find any words or phrases which add to the gloomy picture the poem has already presented.
3   Reconsider your work on the second task. What/who is the poem ultimately about?
4   How do you respond to this poem? What meanings can you find in it, and what is your reaction to them?

59

Commentary

The long sentence is framed by a conditional 'but if' at the beginning, which, for the sentence to be completed, needs a further clause; it comes at the very end with the words 'I don't know'. Both the beginning and end of the sentence, then, express doubt.

In between comes the meat in the sandwich of this 'but if ... don't know' – what is it that the persona does not know about? In a succession of clauses, the persona invents a possible life for a man he did not meet:

◎ did he stand and watch?
◎ lie on the bed?
◎ tell himself this was home?
◎ grin yet shiver?

All of the verbs involve doing nothing physically active, because Bleaney is a sort of prisoner in his room, except when he goes on holiday. Meanwhile, the modifying adjectives 'frigid' and 'fusty' make the scene more depressing, and less neutral. The inclusion of these words influences the reader's perception of how gloomy it all is.

Having speculated on what Bleaney is doing, the persona then moves on to what he might be thinking. This again is not presented neutrally – the word 'dread' is left hanging at the end of a verse, given extra prominence by its rhyme with 'bed'. What Bleaney might be dreading is 'That how we live measures our own nature' – in other words to what extent do our physical surroundings reflect what we are as people? If you live in a 'hired box' then that's what you're worth as a person, you warrant nothing better. Because this is still the same sentence, and the reader is still waiting for the conclusion to the original 'if', there is a growing momentum to the sentence, which is then stopped suddenly by the comma, and the apparent anti-climax of the words 'I don't know'.

So who is the poem ultimately about? In the end, Mr Bleaney is too distant. Too much about him, despite the minor details we know about, has to be guessed. The persona is using him as a yardstick against his own life. Mr Bleaney may not have thought about what this room signifies, but the persona has. The 'dread' really belongs to the persona who has thought himself superior to Mr Bleaney, but now realises that they have an awful lot in common. The reader too is forced to share this dread by the inclusion of 'we' – unless, that is, the reader rejects the whole hypothesis and refuses to be part of the discussion.

A number of possible meanings and responses is possible. Is it Larkin who is pessimistic in this poem? Or is it his persona? Can the two be separated that clearly? Is this a poem of limited relevance, about single men who lived in tawdry digs in the 1950s, or is it more universal, is it claiming to be something about all our lives? Do you as a reader feel included in the poem, or do you stand outside it? Does the persona feel superior to Bleaney and the landlady, if only because he is analysing in a way Bleaney might not have done? These are just some of the questions which arise. As its final words suggest, there is a lot of doubt surrounding this poem.

The work you have done on Mr Bleaney has involved looking at the following:

◉   the importance of titles, openings and endings;
◉   connotation;
◉   the role of a persona in narrating a poem;
◉   how a text can be read as belonging to the time it was written but also needing a response from a modern reader;
◉   the way syntax and stucture can affect the reading of a poem;
◉   the importance of ambiguity in a reading, rather than certainty.

Through exploring these ideas you have investigated some of the attitudes and values which are in the poem.

Robert Browning   *The Patriot*

Some of these same issues will now be addressed in a nineteenth-century poem, *The Patriot* by Robert Browning.

Read the poem carefully twice.

Text   *The Patriot*
An Old Story

I

It was roses, roses, all the way,
    With myrtle mixed in my path like mad:
The house-roofs seemed to heave and sway,
    The church-spires flamed, such flags they had,
A year ago on this very day.

II

The air broke into a mist with bells,
    The old walls rocked with the crowd and cries.
Had I said, 'Good folk, mere noise repels –
    But give me your sun from yonder skies!'
They had answered, 'And afterward, what else?'

III

Alack, it was I who leaped at the sun
    To give it my loving friends to keep!
Nought man could do, have I left undone:
    And you see my harvest, what I reap
This very day, now a year is run.

IV

There's nobody on the house-tops now –
    Just a palsied few at the windows set;
For the best of the sight is, all allow,
    At the Shambles' Gate – or, better yet,
By the very scaffold's foot, I trow.

V

I go in the rain, and, more than needs,
    A rope cuts both my wrists behind;
And I think, by the feel, my forehead bleeds
    For they fling, whoever has a mind,
Stones at me for my year's misdeeds.

VI

Thus I entered, and thus I go!
    In triumphs, people have dropped down dead.
'Paid by the world, what dost thou owe
    Me?' – God might question; now instead,
'Tis God shall repay: I am safer so.

Task

This poem has both a title, *The Patriot*, and a subtitle, *An Old Story*. Both of these phrases carry possible cultural associations; in other words when you read them, you may be aware that they have various possible meanings both for you and for others.

Working in a group if possible, and using reference works such as a dictionary and a dictionary of quotations, make a list of your initial responses to these titles.

Commentary

The main title uses the **definite article** 'the', whereas the subtitle uses the **indefinite article** 'an'. This suggests that the poem is about someone specific (*the* patriot) and yet tells one of a number of stories (*an* old story).

The word 'patriot' derives originally from the Greek word 'patrios', meaning of one's father. A patriot, then, loves the fatherland, but for many readers, certainly within British culture, to be a patriot is not necessarily a good thing. The eighteenth century poet Dryden wrote: 'Never was patriot yet, but was a fool' and Dr Johnson famously wrote that 'Patriotism is the last refuge of a scoundrel'. There is a long tradition of the word being used to suggest either foolishness or cunning – as bald a title as *The Patriot* hints that this poem is not going to end happily.

An Old Story can also be read in different ways. It could refer to the fact that this is a poem set in past times, or it could suggest that it is an old story because it is telling the same old story – in other words, there have been many such stories and they all turn out the same.

Task

Clearly a fictional persona narrates this 'story' – there can be no confusion over whether it is a fictional character or Browning himself, not least because the narrator of the poem is about to be hanged. Write two columns and list:

1   What Browning allows you find out about the actions of this persona/character;
2   What you do not find out but ideally might like to know.

Commentary

The following are some suggested answers to the previous task.

What you find out	What is absent
A year ago he was a hero	What had he done to be so popular?
He received a rapturous reception	Where is the action set?
He tried to help his friends	In what time is the action set?
He is now going to the scaffold	What has he done in the intervening year?
Only a few watch now	Why is he being executed?

In the previous chapter, when looking at the opening of Jane Austen's *Sense and Sensibility*, it was noted that the characters were introduced and settings were geographically and socially located. In addition to these spatial aspects, there were also aspects of time, such as when the action took place and what had gone before. In this poem, this does not happen, creating a sense of unease for the reader; ambiguity and uncertainty are at the very heart of the poem. A short poem is here doing something that a much longer novel cannot do.

To recap, we have seen titles that are ambiguous in their possible responses and a story with serious gaps in it being narrated by a persona whose actions are also surrounded by mystery. As readers, we will probably try to fill in the gaps – is he a soldier returning from war, for instance? – but we cannot be sure.

Task

Although we do not know much about the events surrounding the narrator's past, the way Browning presents his character does allow us to speculate on the patriot's attitudes and values. Using relevant quotations to support your findings, make notes on what you feel are the narrator's main characteristics.

Commentary

When talking about fictional characters, it is important to note that they are not real, they only have characteristics within the framework of the text in which they appear. The best way to explore character is through the author's **characterisation**, the way the characters are presented to us by the author.

One possible reading is that the patriot in this poem is presented as both wise and foolish. When describing the entry to the city, he provides an imaginary conversation with the crowd ('Had I said'). He knows that if he had asked for the sun, they would have offered it and more, and yet it would have been an impossible thing to ask for. He knows that the crowd are fickle, that they will promise anything because they are swept up by the occasion in a way that he is not. And yet for 'my loving friends', friends who he knows will be disloyal, he 'leaped at the sun' and ruined everything. Even as he walks to the scaffold, he is detached enough to know where are the best views of a hanging. His line 'Thus I entered and thus I go!' is resigned rather than bitter, the resignation stressed by the way Browning uses repetition in both vocabulary and syntax. He is presented, then, as someone who knows the world and the people in it. The last lines, as with *Mr Bleaney*, are the ones which require closest attention.

Task

Look at the final verse of the poem. What sort of conclusion does it give to the poem? Although you will probably want to work out what these lines mean, to find answers if you can, consider also the questions that are raised by these lines, and how the way they are written contributes to the discussion. Compare them to the way the poem starts.

Commentary

The opening line of the poem, 'It was roses, roses all the way', is exceptionally rhythmic, with its uncomplicated vocabulary and its repetition. By the end of the poem, things are a good deal more complicated. The verse begins with two end-stopped lines: 'Thus I entered and thus I go!' followed by 'In triumphs, people have dropped down dead.' Both lines carry the suggestion of someone resigned to his fate, aware that triumph and death are always close. The last three lines, however, are much more enigmatic, and the verse form emphasises this, with its more fractured use of lines.

Browning has already used the device of an imaginary piece of speech. Now it is God who 'might' be speaking. There is a sustained metaphor of paying, owing, repaying which runs through the last three lines, but its precise meaning seems elusive. Likewise, 'the world' seems to be placed in comparison to 'God', the physical life versus the afterlife. Does God suggest (in a speech he never makes) that the patriot has enjoyed the pleasures of the physical world and so must now pay his spiritual debt? Apparently not, because 'instead' (of what?) God will 'repay'. Is this meant as a word of revenge, as in 'I'll repay you for this'? And if the patriot is 'safer', safer than what? Safer in the hands of God than of men?

In one sense, the answers to these questions need not bother us; they are the inevitably unsettled thoughts of a man about to be hanged. On the other hand the poem seems to be making a point. While we can quite easily access the attitudes and values of the patriot, it is much harder to say with any real conviction what attitudes and values Browning has. There seem to be plenty of potential ideas about success, fame, public fickleness, patriotism, but they are somehow elusive. This elusiveness tends to be much more possible in poetry than in novels; poems do not require the detailed working out of things that novels generally do. The extent to which you, as reader, like this elusiveness will in part influence your final response to the poem.

Task

Write a short introduction to this poem, an introduction which would be made on a radio programme which specialises in the readings of famous poems. Decide how you would introduce the poem to an audience which likes poetry but does not necessarily know this poem. One key decision for you to make is the extent to which you will go in saying what this poem is 'about'.

Elizabeth Barrett Browning
Sonnet 26 from *Sonnets From the Portuguese*

This section will address an important issue concerning **the writer's context**: to what extent is it useful to know biographical material about an author, and to what extent does such material open up or exclude possible readings? In addressing this question, a conscious choice has to be made – is the biographical material made available before you read the poem, or once you have gained an initial impression? In this case it is before you read the poem, although you should consider whether your responses would be the same if you were given this material afterwards.

The poem to be looked at in this chapter connects with the previous one in that Robert Browning and Elizabeth Barrett Browning were married to each other. While Robert Browning is famous for being a poet, Elizabeth Barrett Browning is famous for being a poet with a romantic life story. The traditional version of this story can be found in many literary reference works. The following details and quotations are taken from the *Everyman Dictionary of Literary Biography* published in 1958.

> 'Very precocious, she read Homer in Greek at the age of eight'. In her teens she fell off a pony, suffering spinal injury which caused her to lie on her back for years. After her mother died, her tyrannical father moved the family to Wimpole Street in London. As early as 14 she was a published writer.
>
> In 1838 her favourite brother drowned, 'a tragic shock which changed her whole life'.
>
> She had already been threatened with lung disease and from that time onwards lived in a darkened room with few visitors. She read widely and in 1844 had two more volumes of poetry published. The poet Robert Browning, 'six years her junior', began to write to her and in 1846 they met. 'They fell in love and decided to elope, in spite of her helpless condition'. Her furious father 'never forgave her and never saw her again'. The elopement 'cured her invalidism' and the marriage was 'ideally happy, she lived to be over 55 and had a son'.
>
> The *Sonnets from the Portuguese*, a deliberately misleading title, making the poems seem like translations, are described in the Everyman Dictionary as being her most famous, and 'the intensely personal utterance of a wife's feelings for her husband'.

What we have so far, then, is a typical picture from Victorian melodrama. A crippled child/woman is kept captive by a tyrannical father, she is heart-broken by the death of a brother, and rescued by a young poet with whom she elopes. With him she finds restored health, ideal love, motherhood, and poetic fame by writing about her love for her husband. In this version of her story, all the key points of reference involve men.

A rather different reading of her life is possible though. In her book *Elizabeth Barrett Browning* (1995), Marjorie Stone points out that the author of *Sonnets from the Portuguese*:

was also the author of a feminist novel-epic (*Aurora Leigh*) which went through over twenty editions between 1857 and 1900. … Victorian reviews of Barrett Browning's works and her impact on other writers indicate that she was widely viewed as a major poet in England and America … from the 1840s up to the 1890s.

Stone also shows that the roots of *Sonnets from the Portuguese* come from her reading of Petrarch and other Italian poets, and that her notebooks contain ideas for love poems dating from well before she met Browning. In this version of the story, Barrett Browning is a much more independent figure, able to be viewed without reference to the men in her life.

For most of this century, critical comments on Barrett Browning linked her, in an inferior way, with her husband. Stone quotes John W. Cunliffe writing in 1908:

> Browning's influence upon his wife is written large on the surface of all her later works, the best thing she ever did, the *Sonnets from the Portuguese* being directly due to his inspiration.

As late as 1983, Margaret Stonyk in *Nineteenth Century English Literature* writes:

> The considerable romance of her life has outlasted her reputation as a poet … once considered for the laureatship but now confined to the servants' quarters in the mansion of literature … *Sonnets from the Portuguese* will always have appreciative if uncritical readers, though their strenuous but inexact language shows the poet at her worst. (The word 'laureatship' refers to the role of Poet Laureat, a sort of official national poet).

What we have here are two versions of her life story and two critical evaluations. Victorians considered her a major poet, good enough to be 'considered for the laureatship'. Modern feminist critics see her as worthy of being re-evaluated as a Victorian feminist writing from her own standpoint rather than her husband's. Sandwiched in time between these positive readings are the negative ones from critics who see her as an adjunct of her husband, writing moderate poems which do not allow her to enter 'the mansion' inhabited by their appointed literary greats.

What this discussion has done so far is to highlight some ways in which context can be seen to affect the way we read texts:

1   **The writer's context** has been seen through the way Barrett Browning's life story has been linked to her poetry.
2   **The text's context** has been seen through the way the poems' origins have been disputed.
3   **The readings context** has been seen through the different critical responses to her work.

In now turning to an example of her work, we can begin to form our own opinions, while always being aware of the ambiguity created by the different readings we have seen already.

Text   *Sonnet 26*

I lived with visions for my company
Instead of men and women, years ago,
And found them gentle mates, nor thought to know
A sweeter music than they played to me.
But soon their trailing purple was not free
Of this world's dust, – their lutes did silent grow,
And I myself grew faint and blind below
Their vanishing eyes. Then THOU didst come ... to be,
Beloved, what they seemed. Their shining fronts,
Their songs, their splendours, (better, yet the same,
As river-water hallowed into fonts)
Met in thee, and from out thee overcame
My soul with satisfaction of all wants –
Because God's gift put man's best dreams to shame.

Task

What evidence can you find in the poem to support the idea that this is a traditional love poem, showing a wife's feelings for her husband?

Commentary

The following commentary gives some ideas to support the above. It is not exhaustive, though, and you will probably have found other ideas.

69

The sonnet is a traditional form for love poetry; in using that form, and in writing a whole sequence of poems in that form, Barrett Browning creates a certain expectation in the reader.

The poem is divided into two parts, a sort of 'before' and 'after'. In the 'before' section, Barrett Browning writes of living with 'visions', and in the 'after' section, of a new life with the man she calls 'THOU'. Although we must be careful not to *assume* that the narrator is the author, there is much to suggest that this is indeed Barrett Browning's own experience being recounted here, and from the first word onwards there is a strong sense of the personal. This, then, is a woman locked away, living with ideas rather than people and for some time happy like this. Her personified 'visions' are 'gentle mates', who play sweet music to her. 'But soon' they begin to be tainted by the 'world's dust'. The regal gowns worn by these once-perfect visions begin to gather dust and lose their perfection. Their music stops, and she begins to grow weak and blind. There is a sense here of fading away, of a private world that sustains her for a while, but cannot last for ever. This fits perfectly with the idea of the Victorian woman who is resourceful and imaginative in her isolation, but longing for something better.

At this point 'THOU' arrives, and his arrival is followed by a row of dots ' ... ', a sort of swoon perhaps. He (Robert Browning?) has existence – 'to be' – whereas the previous visions only 'seemed'. Although he is physical in his presence, he nonetheless assumes a spiritual dimension too. The 'splendours' of her visions all meet in him. He is likened to holy water, but he is better, and he overcomes her 'soul'.

The final line is something of a **paradox**. God in his gifts is superior to anything that humans can dream about, yet in this sense God's gift to her is indeed a perfect man.

Task

Now look at the poem again, this time finding evidence for the view that this is not a traditional love poem, but instead about the escape by a woman from traditional views on love.

Commentary

Although Barrett Browning has used the sonnet form, it can be argued that the form is used not to support a traditional view of love, but ironically to undermine it. The way that the pivotal shift from 'visions' to 'THOU' occurs in the middle of a line, with some interesting **graphological** effects such as capital letters and rows of dots, shows that she is not exactly following the traditional route of a sonnet. Although her rhyme scheme has an 8:6 division, her subject matter has an untidier division. On the one hand she heralds with capital letters the arrival of a lover, yet structurally that arrival comes in the middle of a line.

This sense of things being not necessarily what they seem can be endorsed further by looking at gender-specific references in the poem. Because we know that Barrett Browning, with the luggage of her life story, wrote this poem, there is a temptation to graft that story onto our reading. But the gender of the narrator and the gender of the lover are never specified. Within the sequence of sonnets as a whole, there are many references to the lover as 'he', but here this is not the case. There are, though, two points where gender is specified. In line two we are told that the visions that 'I' have for company are replacements for 'men and women'. But in the final line we are told that it is 'man's' dreams that are shamed by a gift from God. The use of 'man' to refer to both sexes would have been common in Victorian times, but in that case why is it not used earlier? And anyway, as modern readers we bring our own use of language to bear on the way we read. If, therefore, we choose to see that it is specifically male dreams that are shamed by God's gift, some interesting meanings are opened up.

One possible avenue to follow is to do with the way men view women, and the way women view themselves. If God's gift to women is something superior to men's 'best dreams', then perhaps Barrett Browning is referring to sexual pleasure that men traditionally denied in their social constructions of women. In the constructed male view, women required 'gentle mates', 'visions' rather than real sexual partners offering real physical passion. Certainly in Victorian times, sexual fulfilment for women was a taboo subject, but there are suggestions here that Barrett Browning could be talking about physical as well as spiritual 'satisfaction'. After all, it is 'satisfaction of all wants' that she finds in her 'beloved'.

The previous reading of the poem saw Barrett Browning suggesting that she had found an ideal love with a spiritualised man. This reading suggests something different. Although the lover is crucial to what has happened, the real emphasis is not on 'him' but on her. It is not so much that she has been rescued by a man, but that she is a woman who finds her true self in physical love rather than the idealised love found in visions. The potentially erotic language of 'come' 'out thee' suggest that a physical relationship meets her needs far more than her fantasies ever did.

The work on this poem, then, suggests that biographical detail about writers can be helpful in forming *a* reading of a text, but should not be allowed to dominate to such an extent that it provides the *only* reading of a text. Looking at the circumstances of an author's life must not stop us as readers from viewing a text through the circumstances of our own lives. In other words looking at **the writer's context** alone is not enough; we must also explore issues raised by **the reader's context**.

Conclusion

The work you have done in this chapter has used a closely-structured approach to reading poems. Breaking down the exploration of the texts into small units has given you a model for answering the larger, more general questions that you usually find in exams.

The particular focus of this chapter has concentrated on two aspects of reading poetry. One is the nature of the genre itself. This has involved looking at such things as: the importance of titles, openings and endings; connotation; the role of a persona narrating a poem; the way syntax and stucture can affect the reading of a poem. Looking back to the context outline at the beginning of this book, much of this work belongs to what we have called **the language context**.

The second major focus has been on the importance of ambiguity in a reading, rather than certainty. Part of this ambiguity comes from the tension between the way a text can be read as belonging to the time it was written, but at the same time requiring a response from a modern reader. Within this focus, then, this chapter has looked in particular at **the readings context** and **the reader's context**.

The discussion of Barrett Browning's poem has looked at **the writer's context** through the way Barrett Browning's life story has been linked to her poetry and **the text's context** through the way the poem's origins have been disputed.

All of the above has led to the overarching idea that interpretations of poems are not fixed, not 'right', and that provided you are logical and rigorous in your approach, you can argue your own point of view.

Chapter six

Making readings in drama

Plays, novels and poems are very different sorts of literary texts. This can be shown in one way by considering the extent to which they can be read and/or heard. Novels are the most 'readerly' form, usually consumed by individuals alone, and not mediated by anyone else. (An exception would be the 'talking book' or the 'radio reading'.) Poems are the next most 'readerly' form, in that they can be read by an individual alone, but also can be heard in a public recital. Sound is are a key part of poetry: hearing a poem read to you can add to its impact. On the other hand, hearing a poem but not reading it can mean you lose some of the densely-packed meaning which the poem may contain.

A play is the least 'readerly' form. It can be read by an individual, but with difficulty and probably never with full effect. It is best seen and heard in performance, in a production made either for stage or film. Plays and novels both contain fictional characters and plots, but otherwise they have less in common than is sometimes thought, and less in common than is sometimes suggested by the questions that are set in exams. Writing about plays as part of an English course requires a keen awareness of what a drama text is, and how it differs from other forms of writing.

In English courses you are, if writing about plays in exams, *writing about your reading of a work that was written to be seen and heard.* This calls for some pretty sophisticated understanding on your part if you are to show a clear understanding of how the genre of drama works.

The key point here is that stage plays are written to be *performed*, usually in a theatre. They are not meant to be read in the way novels are, by an individual sitting alone. (Although occasionally, plays written for television or radio appear in English courses, on the whole, stage drama has a much higher status in literary study than works written for other media.) If you read a play by yourself at home, or in class with various teachers and students taking the parts, you are not approaching the text in the way that the playwright intended. If you go to see the play on stage, this will undoubtedly be a more 'authentic' experience, but what you have seen is one version, not the definitive theoretical one which often seems to be referred to in examination questions. If you watch a video of a play, you have the advantage of being able to look at the text, and to stop the video when you want; the trouble is, you are not watching a stage version but a version that has been altered to suit the medium of film.

All of this means that studying drama as part of English, while often great fun, can be very challenging. Much of the challenge lies in the fact that drama, especially stage drama, cannot be approached in the way you approach novels. However many readings you may be able to make of a novel or a poem, the text in front of you is always there. With a stage play, nothing at all is fixed: only in a performance does one version of the play come into existence, and you watch it without any written text at all. And this one performance that you see will not be identical to the one the following night, and the one after that.

There are some people, especially those who work in theatre, or teach Theatre Studies, who think that English should keep away from plays altogether – that plays cannot be approached by literary critical methods. But plays, not least Shakespeare's, are compulsory in most English courses. In studying plays, English students must always be aware of what sort of text they are studying, and what they can usefully say about that text. It makes sense, for instance, to write about a performance of a play, or how a play could be performed, or some of the challenges facing actors when they do perform a play. It makes less sense to write about characters in a play as though they are real people with real motivations – an approach which was once very popular in English courses.

This chapter, then, will look at some ways to study and write about plays as part of English courses, by focusing on some aspects of the ways plays work as texts to be realised in performance.

Informing the audience

In its fully-realised version – i.e. in a stage performance – a play tells its story through speech and actions. Stage drama is limited in what it can show; unlike film drama it cannot range widely in a geographical sense. In *Othello*, for instance, the audience can be made aware that the action moves from Venice to Cyprus but, apart from a few different stage props, we still see the same physical space in front of us. (Radio drama, on the other hand, can move freely in space simply because it does not actually show any spaces at all.)

Time is another issue which playwrights must consider. They cannot show everything that happens in the story because, unlike a novel, there is a fixed amount of time available. Anything much more than three hours and the audience will want to go home. This limitation of time means that characters must also be established quickly. Again, unlike a novel, there cannot be a leisurely unfolding of characterisation. This means that stage playwrights have to use certain techniques to suggest space, time, character and events over and above those that are to be physically shown. A big wide world has to be represented on a small stage. One technique of informing the audience about what has happened earlier, in a different place, is to tell them directly. This can be done in an obviously artificial way by having a chorus figure step forward and talk to the audience directly, as happens in *Romeo and Juliet,* where the chorus tells the whole story, both past and future, in a mere fourteen lines, or in *Henry V*, where the Chorus makes more frequent appearances.

The Chorus in *Henry V* is used by Shakespeare to remind the audience that they are just that, an audience, and that they must use their imagination if the play is to work. So at the beginning of Act III, when the action moves to the battlegrounds of France, we are told to:

> Suppose that you have seen
> The well-appoined King at Hampton pier
> Embark his royalty …
> … Follow, follow!
> Grapple your minds to sternage of this navy,
> And leave your England.

Task

Two different methods of giving past information are used by Shakespeare in *Macbeth* and in *The Tempest*. *Macbeth* opens with a very short scene in which three witches plan to meet Macbeth. In the next scene a sergeant, bleeding heavily from his wounds, tells King Duncan and his son Malcolm what has been happening in a battle that is taking place off-stage.

Read the extract carefully and then make notes on the following:

1   What expectations are raised about Macbeth, a character the audience has not yet seen?
2   How might an audience view Duncan and Malcolm in comparison with Macbeth?

Text *Macbeth*

DUNCAN: What bloody man is that? He can report,
　　　As seemeth by his plight, of the revolt
　　　The newest state.
MALCOLM: This is the Sergeant,
　　　Who like a good and hardy soldier fought
　　　'Gainst my captivity: hail brave friend;
　　　Say to the King, the knowledge of the broil,
　　　As thou didst leave it.
CAPTAIN: Doubtful it stood,
　　　As two spent swimmers, that do cling together,
　　　And choke their art. The merciless Macdonwald
　　　(Worthy to be a rebel, for to that
　　　The multiplying villanies of Nature
　　　Do swarm upon him) from the Western Isles
　　　Of kerns and gallowglasses is suppli'd,
　　　And Fortune on his damned quarry smiling,
　　　Show'd like a rebel's whore: but all's too weak:
　　　For brave Macbeth (well he deserves that name)
　　　Disdaining Fortune, with his brandish'd steel,
　　　Which smok'd with bloody execution,
　　　(Like Valour's minion) carv'd out his passage,

Till he fac'd the slave:
Which ne'er shook hands, nor bade farewell to him,
Till he unseam'd him from the nave to th' chops,
And fix'd his head upon our battlements.
DUNCAN: O valiant cousin, worthy gentleman.
CAPTAIN: As whence the sun 'gins his reflection,
Shipwracking storms, and direful thunders break:
So from that spring, whence comfort seem'd to come,
Discomfort swells. Mark King of Scotland, mark,
No sooner Justice had, with Valour arm'd,
Compell'd these skipping kerns to trust their heels,
But the Norweyan Lord, surveying vantage,
With furbish'd arms and new supplies of men,
Began a fresh assault.
DUNCAN: Dismay'd not this our Captains, Macbeth and Banquo?
CAPTAIN: Yes, as sparrows eagles; or the hare the lion:
If I say sooth, I must report they were
As cannons overcharg'd with double cracks,
So they doubly redoubled strokes upon the foe:
Except they meant to bathe in reeking wounds,
Or memorise another Golgotha,
I cannot tell: but I am faint,
My gashes cry for help.
DUNCAN: So well thy words become thee, as thy wounds,
They smack of honour both: go get him surgeons.

Now look at the way Shakespeare manages past events in *The Tempest*. In the following extract, Prospero, who lives on an island with his daughter Miranda, argues with Caliban. Caliban, half man half fish, was on the island before Prospero arrived. In the following extract, Prospero says why he has treated Caliban the way he has.

Task

Read the extract carefully and then make notes on the following:

1   What do we learn about the past from this extract?
2   What different readings of the past events are possible here?

Text *The Tempest*

CALIBAN: I must eat my dinner.
This island's mine, by Sycorax my mother,
Which thou tak'st from me. When thou cam'st first,
Thou strok'st me, and made much of me; wouldst give me
Water with berries in't; and teach me how
To name the bigger light, and how the less,
That burn by day and night: and then I lov'd thee,
And show'd thee all the qualities o' th' isle,
The fresh springs, brine-pits, barren place and fertile:
Curs'd be I that did so! All the charms
Of Sycorax, toads, beetles, bats, light on you!
For I am all the subjects that you have,
Which first was mine own King: and here you sty me
In this hard rock, whiles you do keep from me
The rest o' th' island.

PROSPERO: Thou most lying slave,
Whom stripes may move, not kindness! I have us'd thee,
Filth as thou art, with human care; and lodg'd thee
In mine own cell, till thou didst seek to violate
The honour of my child.

CALIBAN: O ho, O ho! would't had been done!
Thou didst prevent me; I had peopled else
This isle with Calibans.

MIRANDA: Abhorred slave,
Which any print of goodness wilt not take,
Being capable of all ill! I pitied thee,
Took pains to make thee speak, taught thee each hour
One thing or other: when thou didst not, savage,
Know thine own meaning, but wouldst gabble like
A thing most brutish, I endow'd thy purposes
With words that made them known. But thy vile race,
Though thou didst learn, had that in't which good natures
Could not abide to be with; therefore wast thou
Deservedly confin'd into this rock,
Who hadst deserv'd more than a prison.

CALIBAN: You taught me language; and my profit on't
Is, I know how to curse. The red plague rid you
For learning me your language!

Commentary

It is worth noting to begin with that the 'narrator' from Macbeth has just left the battlefield and on stage should be a striking figure, covered in plenty of stage blood. There are likely to be noises of the battle still going on, and we know that Malcolm has been fighting in it. There is no textual mention of Duncan taking part, although how he is dressed on stage will give the audience major clues as to whether they are to think Duncan is a soldier king or not. There is no absolute answer here – it rests with the director, and the overall conception of the play.

Macbeth is placed at the centre of the sergeant's narrative, which is exceptionally poetic and imaginative for one who has just left the battle severely wounded. Taking this situation too literally, though, is to miss the point. The purpose of the sergeant is essentially twofold: one is to show some of the violence of a battle that cannot be shown; we cannot see a man being opened up from the stomach to the jawbone, we can only hear about it. The second is to place Macbeth centre stage, to make it clear that without him the battle would be lost. Once the sergeant has served his **dramatic purpose**, he is not needed any more.

This study of dramatic purpose, an analysis of what a character through appearance, words and actions contributes to the telling of the story as a whole, is one very effective way in which to write about plays. What the sergeant tells us about Macbeth is that he is fearless and violent, a peerless soldier who has allowed Duncan to resist the rebels who threaten his throne. All of this is conveyed in a brief time on stage. Horror and exultation are mixed in equal measure; we want to see this superhero for ourselves.

In the extract from *The Tempest*, there is a three-way exchange; in the *Macbeth* extract, the sergeant speaks for most of the time. Both extracts are connected through the use of 'intense' situations. The sergeant is bleeding and breathless, whereas in *The Tempest*, there is a fierce argument, with curses and strong threats. Caliban on the one hand, Prospero and Miranda on the other, are convinced they are justified, and in justifying themselves they provide details of what has happened before the action of the play began. So Caliban talks of the island being his, of initially kind treatment from Prospero, of each educating the other. But all that has changed and Caliban is now a 'slave', a word used by both Prospero and Caliban. The reason for the change is that Caliban attempted to rape Miranda, the person who had taught him how to speak. Now, says Caliban, he will use the power of speech to curse and, presumably, rebel.

There is, in this argument, more scope for ambiguity than there is with the sergeant in *Macbeth*. A **post-colonial reading**, for example, could see Caliban in a sympathetic light, someone who is dispossessed, forced to speak English, enslaved to a conquering culture in a similar way to Friday in *Robinson Crusoe* (see chapter 4). A feminist reading could focus on the attempted rape of Miranda, as well as her own relative enslavement to the will of her father. This argument, about past grudges, not only provides intensity on stage, but it also provides different perspectives for an audience to consider.

Peter Shaffer in his play *Amadeus* (1980) explores the jealousy of a lesser composer, Salieri, towards the genius of the composer Mozart. In a fictional drama, based on the lives of real people, Shaffer tells how Salieri sets out to ruin his rival by poisoning his reputation. In his character list, Shaffer mentions two 'Venticelli' whom he describes as 'little winds: purveyors of information, gossip and rumour'. At regular intervals during the play these two Venticelli, essentially indistinguishable from each other, provide the audience with information, but in a rather more oblique way than the sergeant does in Macbeth. Here they are gossiping about the young Mozart.

Task

Work out responses to the following questions:

1 How does Salieri simulate typical gossip here?
2 What information are we given about Mozart here?
3 How does Shaffer characterise Mozart here, even though he is not seen?

(The words **characterise/characterisation** refer to the way an author presents characters, rather than the characteristics that the characters display.)

SALIERI: Where does he live?
VENTICELLO 1: Peter Platz.
VENTICELLO 2: Number eleven.
VENTICELLO 1: The landlady is Madam Weber.
VENTICELLO 2: A real bitch.
VENTICELLO 1: Takes in lodgers, and has a tribe of daughters.

VENTICELLO 2: Mozart is one of them.
VENTICELLO 1: Constanze.
VENTICELLO 2: Flighty little piece.
VENTICELLO 1: Her mother's pushing marriage.
VENTICELLO 2: His father isn't!
VENTICELLO 1: Daddy is worried sick.
VENTICELLO 2: Writes him every day.

Commentary

Gossip is often perceived as being slight, insubstantial talk, and that view is simulated here by the rapid delivery of little snippets of talk and information. Facts, such as numbers of houses and names of people, are mixed with opinions, such as the landlady being 'a real bitch'. The Venticelli, like the bleeding sergeant, have a clear dramatic purpose.

We learn that Mozart has lodgings; we know the address; we know that the landlady has daughters, one of whom, Constanze, is having an affair of some sort with Mozart. Her mother approves, his father disapproves. Such is the information, which is all pretty obvious. How Shaffer is characterising Mozart, though, requires more perception on the part of the audience as they hear this rapid, probably stage-whispered, gossip.

Shaffer has chosen to characterise Mozart in a certain way. It would appear that for all his musical genius, Mozart is naïve in the ways of the world. He is being manipulated by the landlady into marrying one of her many daughters, who is herself aware of what is going on. Mozart's father has a dominant role in his life but, despite writing every day, lives in another city; he cannot stop what is going to happen. Mozart is doomed to a problematic marriage, and to the disapproval of his father which will make things worse.

What Shaffer has done, then, in this short scene taking no more than a minute of stage time is:

◎   suggest a courtship between Mozart and his future wife;
◎   hint at trouble to come;
◎   characterise Mozart as naïve and vulnerable.

Actors and directors

It was noted at the opening of this chapter that however many readings you may be able to make of a novel or a poem, the text in front of you is always there. With a stage play, though, nothing at all is fixed: only in a performance does one version of the play come into existence. As a student of a play text you can comment on potential readings of a play, but must always be aware that these depend upon how it is staged.

A further challenge faces you when you study a play. Presumably you will read and/or see the play a number of times, yet, because you are having to write about it as a play to be performed, you also have to consider the fact that an audience (assuming they too are not students of the play) are seeing it for the first and only time. All the knowledge you have from knowing the play well has to be tempered by an awareness that an audience has none of this knowledge.

The Seagull (1896), by the Russian playwright Anton Chekhov, begins with the following lines. The two characters enter the stage on their way back from a walk.

MEDVEDENKO: Why do you always wear black?
MASHA: I'm in mourning for my life. I'm unhappy.

Some plays begin with lines suggesting that the characters are already talking and we join them somewhere in the middle. Not these though; Medvedenko's question seems to come from nothing that has gone before.

Task

1   Make some notes on how this exchange could be performed; try to come up with at least two versions. If working in a group, direct two of the group as actors of your different versions.

In arriving at your version, consider some of the following:

◎   Do they walk on stage together, or one after the other? In which case who follows whom?

- How long are they on stage before they begin to talk?
- Is Medvedenko serious, irritated, or what, when he asks the question?
- Is Masha being serious or flippant?
- Her reply is in two parts. Does she keep the same tone of voice for both?

2   Now consider the following extra information about the play and these two characters.

- Chekhov described the play as a comedy.
- Medvedenko is a schoolteacher who is in love with Masha. She however loves somebody else. She also drinks a great deal and takes snuff. Eventually they marry, and live together unhappily.

Does this information now make you favour one of your versions in particular?

3   *The Seagull* was written in Russian, so there are several translations available with slightly different wordings. Here are two other versions of these lines:

MEDVEDENKO: Why is it you always wear black?
MASHA: Because I'm in mourning for my life. I'm unhappy.
                                        (Norton edition)

MEDVEDENKO: Why do you always wear black?
MASHA: I am in mourning for my life. I am unhappy.

Are all these versions essentially the same, or does each one create a slightly different effect?

Commentary

Various interpretations of these lines are possible. If Medvedenko and Masha come on stage together, and each speaks the lines with the utmost seriousness, then it is possible to establish a mood which is sober and sombre. Yet however Masha speaks her lines, they border on the over-dramatic. She is, after all, only out on a walk.

Once we know that Chekhov intends the play to be a comedy, we might be tempted to play the lines a lot less seriously. If Medvedenko trails after Masha, complaining to her in a wheedling voice, her lines can be delivered in such a way that she knows she is being melodramatic, and just doing it to annoy. Even if she seems perfectly serious, the actress may slur the words, suggesting she has been drinking – and so make the predominant mood one of comedy.

A third possibility is that the exchange hovers somewhere between both moods, making the audience see both humour and pathos in the situation. Certainly, the more you know about what is going to happen later, the more you can shape an interpretation which will be consistent.

Although the three translations are nearly the same, each is subtly different. The first one, by Michael Frayn, is the most informal and seems more attuned to what a modern audience might expect.

Although some dramatists use stage notes to indicate their views on how to interpret their plays, essentially a drama text has only speech and no narrative. This means that when you are analysing things like assumptions and values contained within a text, you have less that is prescribed for you and more room for your own interpretations.

The dramatisation of eavesdropping in Shakespeare

So far, this chapter has looked at the way plays can be studied. One way to approach the study of Shakespeare, especially for a coursework assignment, is to focus on a specific aspect of **dramatisation** in a play or even better in different plays. As an example, this section will look at the use Shakespeare makes of eavesdropping in two different sorts of play. Just as the word 'characterisation' refers to how an author devises and presents characters, so the word 'dramatisation' refers to the way writers construct and shape their plays (rather than what the play is about in terms of theme/plot).

The word 'eavesdropping' comes from the idea of standing under the eaves of a house, the place where the water dropped, and thus being close enough to the wall to listen. Although we all understand the idea of eavesdropping, it is in fact pretty rare in real spoken contexts. We may sometimes, much to the embarrassment of all involved, stumble into a conversation we are not meant to hear, and we may sometimes overhear a conversation in an adjacent room, but it is unlikely that we place ourselves hidden from view so that we can overhear with such deliberate intent. Indeed to do so would be considered to be spying, and it is probably within the world of espionage that eavesdropping is most common, through the use of electronic surveillance rather than physical proximity. Eaves-dropping, then, belongs more to the world of drama than to actual spoken discourse; it is a convenient way for a dramatist to shape action.

Eavesdropping, in terms of a play, involves a relationship between the action on stage and the audience watching it. In one sense, the audience of all plays are themselves eavesdropping on the lives and conversations of a group of hitherto unknown strangers, simply by watching the action without being 'seen' by the characters. When the play itself then contains examples of eavesdropping, these only work if the audience knows what is going on, and at least one of the characters does not. The effect of this can vary; in the two examples to be looked at here, the first shows dramatic tension, action, and surprise the second shows comedy and character development.

Eavesdropping in **Hamlet**

Inevitably in approaching specific parts of a play or plays, a certain amount of plot has to be outlined to place the example in context. The first example comes from *Hamlet*.

Plot summary

Hamlet, believing his father to have been murdered by his uncle, who has subsequently married Hamlet's mother, decides to behave as though mad so that he can prove his suspicions. Polonius, a courtier and the father of Hamlet's girlfriend, is not convinced that Hamlet is mad, so arranges with the Queen, Hamlet's mother, to eavesdrop on a conversation between mother and son. The audience does not know whether the Queen knows about the murder of her first husband or not, but they do know that Polonius is hidden behind a curtain, or arras, listening to the conversation, and that the Queen knows this too. The only person who does not know about the eavesdropping is Hamlet.

Task

Read the following extract, preferably aloud in a class or group. You will need to do this at least twice.

85

Text *Hamlet*

Scene IV   The Queen's Apartment

Enter QUEEN *and* POLONIUS

POLONIUS: He will come straight. Look you lay home to him;
　　　Tell him his pranks have been too broad to bear with,
　　　And that your Grace hath screen'd and stood between
　　　Much heat and him. I'll silence me e'en here.
　　　Pray you, be round with him.
HAMLET: [*Within*.] Mother, mother, mother!
QUEEN:　　　　　　　　　　　　　I'll warrant you;
　　　Fear me not. Withdraw, I hear him coming.
　　　　　　[POLONIUS *hides behind the arras.*

Enter HAMLET

HAMLET: Now, mother, what's the matter?
QUEEN: Hamlet, thou hast thy father much offended.
HAMLET: Mother, you have my father much offended.
QUEEN: Come, come, you answer with an idle tongue.
HAMLET: Go, go, you question with a wicked tongue.
QUEEN: Why, how now, Hamlet!
HAMLET:　　　　　　　　　　　What's the matter now?
QUEEN: Have you forgot me?
HAMLET:　　　　　　　　　　　No, by the rood, not so:
　　　You are the queen, your husband's brother's wife;
　　　And, – would it were not so! – you are my mother.
QUEEN: Nay then, I'll set those to you that can speak.
HAMLET: Come, come, and sit you down; you shall not budge;
　　　You go not, till I set you up a glass
　　　Where you may see the inmost part of you.
QUEEN: What wilt thou do? thou wilt not murder me?
　　　Help, help, ho!
POLONIUS: [*Behind*.] What, ho! help! help! help!
HAMLET: [*Draws*.] How now! a rat? Dead, for a ducat, dead!
　　　　　　　　　　[*Makes a pass through the arras.*
POLONIUS: [*Behind*.] O! I am slain.
QUEEN: O me! what hast thou done?
HAMLET: Nay, I know not: is it the king?
QUEEN: O! what a rash and bloody deed is this!
HAMLET: A bloody deed! almost as bad, good mother,

As kill a king, and marry with his brother.
QUEEN: As kill a king!
HAMLET: Ay, lady, 'twas my word.
[*Lifts up the arras and discovers* POLONIUS.]
[*To* POLONIUS.] Thou wretched, rash, intruding fool, farewell!
I took thee for thy better;

Still in groups, if possible, make notes on the following:

1   In what ways does this extract contain elements of shock for the
     audience, even though they know that Polonius is eavesdrop-
     ping?
2   When you have worked out your responses to question 1, now
     consider how this extract could be staged. Pay particular atten-
     tion to the physical placing of the characters on stage and their
     movements as the lines are spoken. Try to come up with alterna-
     tive suggestions, to help you reinforce the idea that the text is
     not fixed in how it works, and that there are several ways of
     interpreting it.

Read the commentary below when you have completed your answers.

Commentary

There are at least two ways in which the audience can be shocked
here. The most obvious involves the sudden and apparently heartless
killing of Polonius. Hamlet, who has not been much of a man of
action so far in the play, suddenly launches himself at an unknown
eavesdropper, not only killing him, but saying gratuitously off-hand
words at the same time. He presumes that he has possibly killed 'the
king', but does not know for sure because he cannot see his victim.
Note here how the language of the play makes some of the decisions
for the director. However the scene is arranged on stage, Hamlet
cannot be allowed to see whom he has killed until he lifts the curtain.

There is little more sympathy from Hamlet for Polonius when
his body is discovered. He may be seen by Hamlet as a spy, but at the
same time he is, or was, his prospective father-in-law. Some productions play this part of the scene as almost comic, but it is uneasy
comedy when death comes so cheaply.

A sense of shock also comes at the highly-charged moment between the stabbing and the discovery of who has been stabbed. The staging of this brief moment is crucial to its effect, but, as can be seen on the page, there is a lot going on here. Polonius says 'I am slain', an indicator of death that is common in Shakespeare, but which none-theless often makes modern audiences laugh. However, without having this fact asserted for us, how can we know that he has not suffered a mere scratch?

With the death of someone established – we know who, the Queen knows who, but Hamlet does not – there is a pause in the action. Instead of Hamlet rushing to find out whom he has murdered, he uses the moment to accuse his mother of complicity in the murder of her first husband. Throughout this short extract, he has echoed his mother's words, so when she accuses him of 'a rash and bloody deed', he picks up on the words 'bloody deed' and suggests that she has helped kill the King. Her words 'As kill a king' are potentially hugely significant for the audience as they attempt to follow the play. One of the questions they have wanted the answer to for some time is: did the Queen know about/take part in the original murder? Now, at the very moment when the truth can come out, it is shrouded in ambi-guity. Do her words express amazed shock at the fact that her former husband was murdered, or do they express shock that she has been discovered? There can be no definitive answer, although the actress performing the role can give substantial clues. The main point to note here is that this time, it is the audience and Hamlet who are in the dark. Hamlet has his suspicions, but he is emotionally involved. The audience, who have known about Polonius eavesdropping, are momentarily put into a position of not knowing. The question is for the time being forgotten as Hamlet discovers whom he has really killed.

Hamlet is a tragedy, a serious play. Although this scene has the potential for some comedy, it would be rather uncomfortable for the audience. In terms of the eavesdropping, the audience begins this scene in a position of knowing more than the main character. But even before Hamlet discovers what the audience already know, that he has killed Polonius, Shakespeare manipulates the audience in a different direction, this time leaving them in a position of not knowing. This sense of keeping the audience in the dark over impor-tant issues allows Shakespeare to increase the tension and uncertainty in a play dealing with very serious concerns.

Each production will give a different slant on such matters; if you have the opportunity to see the play performed on stage or film, your written response could refer to how a specific production manages this scene.

The dramatic device of eavesdropping is used, then, not only to enable events to proceed within the play but also to place the audience, through what they know and what they do not know, as active figures in the drama. As a comparison to the tragedy of *Hamlet*, we can now explore the role of the audience in a **comedy**.

Eavesdropping in Much Ado About Nothing

The title *Much Ado About Nothing* signalled to an Elizabethan audience a pun which is no longer obvious to modern audiences. The words 'nothing' and 'noting' would have been pronounced in much the same way in Elizabethan times. So while on the one hand Shakespeare seems to be indicating that his play is about nothing in particular – in much the same way as he does with the title *As you Like It* – he is also suggesting that 'noting', or eavesdropping, is to be a central feature of his play.

An essential ingredient of comedy involves the audience and what it knows. Usually the audience knows more than at least some of the characters. This knowledge can be to do with events and actions, but can also involve knowledge about the characters themselves; the audience will often have been made aware of certain psychological traits which the characters themselves do not fully recognise.

Whereas tragedy involves death and mystery, it is more likely that a comedy will involve characters at various levels of misunderstanding, with the audience knowing more than the characters and sometimes everything. An alert audience, who have kept up with the often intricate patterns of who knows what, gain pleasure from their own knowledge and the gradual dawning on characters of what the audience have known all along.

The background to the extract to be studied is as follows:

Benedick has loudly asserted that he will never marry. His three friends Leonato, an old man, Don Pedro and Claudio, set themselves the challenge to persuade Benedick that he is in love with Beatrice, a woman with whom he has done nothing but argue since the play began. The audience already knows that Benedick has once had some sort of relationship with Beatrice, and that their constant arguing may suggest that they still have a keen interest in each other.

Benedick has just been alone on stage saying why he will never marry. At the approach of the three men, he decides to hide, rather than put up with their company. They, however, know he is there, and they know he will overhear their conversation. Their plan is simple; knowing that Benedick will listen to a conversation about himself, they role-play a scene in which they describe Beatrice's 'love' for Benedick and his cruelty to her.

So in terms of knowledge the following applies:

Benedick – knows nothing about the plot to make him love Beatrice, and has persuaded himself he will never marry. He does not know that his friends know he is hiding.

Leonato/Don Pedro/Claudio – know Benedick is hiding. They like the idea of his being involved with Beatrice, but on the level of blokish fun rather than seeing their real affinity.

Audience – can see Benedick in hiding, know the plans of the three men, suspect that Benedick does indeed love Beatrice.

Task

Read the extract below and then consider the tasks which follow. Each of them gives you an idea of possible ways to approach studying and writing about drama. These tasks have been devised to encourage you to focus very much on stage action, while at the same time maintaining the idea that there are always multiple possibilities in the way we approach texts. This means that there is no commentary with this section of the chapter.

Text *Much Ado About Nothing*

DON PEDRO: Come hither
    Leonato. What was it you told me of today, that your niece Beatrice
    was in love with Signor Benedick?
CLAUDIO: [*Aside*] O ay, stalk on, stalk on, the fowl sits. – I did never
    think that lady would have loved any man.
LEONATO: No nor I neither; but most wonderful that she should dote
    so on Signor Benedick, whom she hath in all outward behaviours
    seemed ever to abhor.

BENEDICK: [*Aside*] Is't possible? Sits the wind in that corner?

LEONATO: By my troth my lord, I cannot tell what to think of it; but that she loves him with an enraged affection – it is past the infinite of thought.

DON PEDRO: May be she doth but counterfeit.

CLAUDIO: Faith, like enough.

LEONATO: O God, counterfeit? There was never counterfeit of passion came so near the life of passion as she discovers it.

DON PEDRO: Why, what effects of passion shows she?

CLAUDIO: [*To Don Pedro and Leonato*] Bait the hook well, this fish will bite.

LEONATO: What effects, my lord? She will sit you – you heard my daughter tell you how.

CLAUDIO: She did indeed.

DON PEDRO: How, how pray you? You amaze me. I would have thought her spirit had been invincible against all assaults of affection.

LEONATO: I would have sworn it had, my lord, especially against Benedick.

BENEDICK: [*Aside*] I should think this a gull, but that the white-bearded fellow speaks it; knavery cannot sure hide himself in such reverence.

CLAUDIO: [*To Don Pedro and Leonato*] He hath ta'en th'infection; hold it up.

DON PEDRO: Hath she made her affection known to Benedick?

LEONATO: No, and swears she never will – that's her torment.

CLAUDIO: 'Tis true indeed, so your daughter says. 'Shall I,' says she, 'that have so oft encountered him with scorn, write to him that I love him?'

LEONATO: This says she now when she is beginning to write to him; for she'll be up twenty times a night, and there will she sit in her smock till she have writ a sheet of paper – my daughter tells us all.

CLAUDIO: Now you talk of a sheet of paper, I remember a pretty jest your daughter told us of.

LEONATO: O, when she had writ it and was reading it over, she found Benedick and Beatrice between the sheet?

CLAUDIO: That.

LEONATO: O, she tore the letter into a thousand halfpence; railed at herself that she should be so immodest to write to one that she knew would flout her. 'I measure him,' says she, 'by my own spirit; for I should flout him if he writ to me; yea though I love him, I should.'

CLAUDIO: Then down upon her knees she falls, weeps, sobs, beats her heart, tears her hair, prays, curses – 'O sweet Benedick! God give me patience.'

LEONATO: She doth indeed – my daughter says so. And the ecstasy hath so much overborne her that my daughter is sometime afeard she will do a desperate outrage to herself. It is very true.

DON PEDRO: It were good that Benedick knew of it by some other, if she will not discover it.

CLAUDIO: To what end? He would make but a sport of it and torment the poor lady worse.

DON PEDRO: An he should, it were an alms to hang him. She's an excellent sweet lady, and, out of all suspicion, she is virtuous.

CLAUDIO: And she is exceeding wise.

DON PEDRO: In every thing but in loving Benedick.

LEONATO: O my lord, wisdom and blood combating in so tender a body, we have ten proofs to one that blood hath the victory. I am sorry for her, as I have just cause, being her uncle and her guardian.

DON PEDRO: I would she had bestowed this dotage on me. I would have daffed all other respects and made her half myself. I pray you tell Benedick of it, and hear what 'a will say.

LEONATO: Were it good think you?

CLAUDIO: Hero thinks surely she will die; for she says she will die, if he love her not; and she will die ere she make her love known; and she will die if he woo her, rather than she will bate one breath of her accustomed crossness.

DON PEDRO: She doth well. If she should make tender of her love, 'tis very possible he'll scorn it; for the man, as you know all, hath a contemptible spirit.

CLAUDIO: He is a very proper man.

DON PEDRO: He hath indeed a good outward happiness.

CLAUDIO: Before God, and in my mind, very wise.

DON PEDRO: He doth indeed show some sparks that are like wit.

CLAUDIO: And I take him to be valiant.

DON PEDRO: As Hector, I assure you; and in the managing of quarrels you may say he is wise, for either he avoids them with great discretion, or undertakes them with a most Christian-like fear.

LEONATO: If he do fear God, 'a must necessarily keep peace; if he break the peace, he ought to enter into a quarrel with fear and trembling.

DON PEDRO: And so will he do; for the man doth fear God, howsoever it seems not in him by some large jests he will make. Well, I am sorry for your niece. Shall we go seek Benedick, and tell him of her love?

CLAUDIO: Never tell him, my lord; let her wear it out with good counsel.

LEONATO: Nay that's impossible, she may wear her heart out first.

DON PEDRO: Well, we will hear further of it by your daughter; let it cool the while. I love Benedick well, and I could wish he would modestly examine himself, to see how much he is unworthy so good a lady.

LEONATO: My lord, will you walk? Dinner is ready.

CLAUDIO: [*Aside*] If he do not dote on her upon this, I will never trust my expectation.

1   Work out a way, or better still, different ways, of staging this scene. Ideally, work as a group, first reading through the script and then attempting to stage it for the whole class, using whatever props are available in the room. If working on your own, you will have to work more hypothetically, but this is still possible. Once you have worked out your staging (or stagings) of this scene, write out the ideas which lie behind your conception of it. You might include some or all of the following:

◎   how you wish to present a comic effect;

◎   how you intend to show Benedick (a) as hidden to the others, so he thinks but (b) seen by the others who know where he is and (c) at times visible to the audience;

◎   how you will differentiate the performances of the three friends.

2   Although the text contains no explicit stage directions, the conversation itself provides many indications of how the actors should perform their parts. Bearing in mind that the three friends are acting out a sort of play-within-a-play, albeit one they are making up as they go along, prepare a detailed set of guidelines for each of the three roles, suggesting to the actors how their performance of the role could be delivered.

3   This task involves a more thorough knowledge of the whole play, and could be used as a coursework submission. Although *Much Ado About Nothing* is ultimately a comedy, it makes some serious points about the nature of relationships between lovers. In so doing, it sets up a contrast between two very different relationships; the idealised but flawed relationship between Claudio

and Hero, and the more conflicting but essentially profound relationship between Benedick and Beatrice. Explore the ways in which Shakespeare uses eavesdropping in his presentation of each relationship, showing how the way characters react to what they hear, or what is reported to them as being overheard, contributes to Shakespeare's overall presentation of relationships between lovers.

Oliver Goldsmith   *She Stoops to Conquer*

The following section will look closely at a larger extract of a play. It will indicate some of the ways in which you can write about drama texts, and also explore some of the ways you can detect the attitudes and values which plays contain, and the ambiguity which is at the centre of many play texts.

She Stoops to Conquer was written by Oliver Goldsmith and first performed in 1773. It has a subtitle, *The Mistakes of a Night*. Both titles contain considerable clues about the play. The subtitle in particular indicates that this play is a comedy, with humour as one of its primary aims. Just because a play is a comedy, though, does not mean that it is without ideological issues; indeed much of the best comic writing, including television situation comedy, explores through humour the attitudes and values held by characters representing social groups and classes.

Task

Read the following extract, taken from the opening of the play, preferably aloud in a class or group. You will need to do this at least twice. Still in groups, if possible, make notes on the following:

1   Comment on the names used for the various fictional people who are referred to. What do they tell you about these people?
2   Drama, by definition, has to involve conflict. What is the nature of the conflict seen here?
3   Is Goldsmith neutral in his presentation of the conflict or does he through his manipulation of dialogue/action lead the audience to take sides?

If possible, compare your ideas with others', and only then consult the commentary which follows.

Text *She Stoops to Conquer*

Scene, a chamber in an old-fashioned house

Enter MRS. HARDCASTLE *and* MR. HARDCASTLE

MRS. HARDCASTLE: I vow, Mr. Hardcastle, you're very particular. Is there a creature in the whole country but ourselves, that does not take a trip to town now and then, to rub off the rust a little? There's the two Miss Hoggs, and our neighbour, Mrs. Grigsby, go to take a month's polishing every winter.

HARDCASTLE: Ay, and bring back vanity and affectation to last them the whole year. I wonder why London cannot keep its own fools at home! In my time, the follies of the town crept slowly among us, but now they travel faster than a stage-coach. Its fopperies come down, not only as inside passengers, but in the very basket.

MRS. HARDCASTLE: Ay, *your* times were fine times indeed; you have been telling us of *them* for many a long year. Here we live in an old rumbling mansion, that looks for all the world like an inn, but that we never see company. Our best visitors are old Mrs. Oddfish, the curate's wife, and little Cripplegate, the lame dancing-master: And all our entertainment your old stories of Prince Eugene and the Duke of Marlborough. I hate such old-fashioned trumpery.

HARDCASTLE: And I love it. I love every thing that's old: old friends, old times, old manners, old books, old wines; and, I believe, Dorothy, *[taking her hand]* you'll own I have been pretty fond of an old wife.

MRS. HARDCASTLE: Lord, Mr. Hardcastle, you're for ever at your Dorothy's, and your old wife's. You may be a Darby, but I'll be no Joan, I promise you. I'm not so old as you'd make me, by more than one good year. Add twenty to twenty, and make money of that.

HARDCASTLE: Let me see; twenty added to twenty, makes just fifty and seven.

MRS. HARDCASTLE: It's false, Mr. Hardcastle: I was but twenty when I was brought to bed of Tony, that I had by Mr. Lumpkin, my first husband; and he's not come to years of discretion yet.

HARDCASTLE: Nor ever will, I dare answer for him. Ay, you have taught him finely.

MRS. HARDCASTLE: No matter, Tony Lumpkin has a good fortune. My son is not to live by his learning. I don't think a boy wants much learning to spend fifteen hundred a year.

HARDCASTLE: Learning, quotha! a mere composition of tricks and mischief.

MRS. HARDCASTLE: Humour, my dear: nothing but humour. Come, Mr. Hardcastle, you must allow the boy a little humour.

HARDCASTLE: I'd sooner allow him an horse-pond. If burning the footmen's shoes, frighting the maids, and worrying the kittens, be humour, he has it. It was but yesterday he fastened my wig to the back of my chair, and when I went to make a bow, I popt my bald head in Mrs. Frizzle's face.

MRS. HARDCASTLE: And am I to blame? The poor boy was always too sickly to do any good. A school would be his death. When he comes to be a little stronger, who knows what a year or two's Latin may do for him?

HARDCASTLE: Latin for him! A cat and fiddle. No, no, the ale-house and the stable are the only schools he'll ever go to.

MRS. HARDCASTLE: Well, we must not snub the poor boy now, for I believe we shan't have him long among us. Any body that looks in his face may see he's consumptive.

HARDCASTLE: Ay, if growing too fat be one of the symptoms.

MRS. HARDCASTLE: He coughs sometimes.

HARDCASTLE: Yes, when his liquor goes the wrong way.

MRS. HARDCASTLE: I'm actually afraid of his lungs.

HARDCASTLE: And truly so am I; for he sometimes whoops like a speaking trumpet – [*Tony hallooing behind the Scenes*] – O there he goes – a very consumptive figure, truly.

Enter TONY, *crossing the Stage*

MRS. HARDCASTLE: Tony, where are you going, my charmer? Won't you give Papa and I a little of your company, lovee?

TONY: I'm in haste, Mother, I cannot stay.

MRS. HARDCASTLE: You shan't venture out this raw evening, my dear: You look most shockingly.

TONY: I can't stay, I tell you. The Three Pigeons expects me down every moment. There's some fun going forward.

HARDCASTLE: Ay; the ale-house, the old place; I thought so.

MRS. HARDCASTLE: A low, paltry set of fellows.

TONY: Not so low neither. There's Dick Muggins the exciseman, Jack Slang the horse doctor, little Aminadab that grinds the music box, and Tom Twist that spins the pewter platter.

MRS. HARDCASTLE: Pray, my dear, disappoint them for one night at least.

TONY: As for disappointing *them,* I should not so much mind; but I can't abide to disappoint *myself.*

MRS. HARDCASTLE: [*Detaining him*]: You shan't go.

TONY: I will, I tell you.

MRS. HARDCASTLE: I say you shan't.
TONY: We'll see which is strongest, you or I.

[*Exit hauling her out*]

Commentary

Many of the names of characters referred to but not seen are verbal
jokes. Mrs Oddfish, Cripplegate, Tom Twist and others are invented to
make the audience laugh. Tony Lumpkin, as a name, also suggests
what the character is, as seen both by mother and stepfather. The
suffix 'kin' means little, and he is little to his mother. To his stepfather
though he is huge, a 'lump'. Tony is also referred to by his mother as
'my charmer', but charm he obviously lacks.

Hardcastle, on the other hand, sounds more solid and resilient.
Note that he calls his wife Dorothy, but she calls him Mr Hardcastle,
suggesting an inequality in their relationship. Using naming systems
to indicate ideas to the audience is a common device in drama, especially comedy.

Among the conflicts you may have found are: the conflict
between old and new; country life versus town life; old things versus
fashion; insight versus parental indulgence. In each case it is the first
of the two which belongs to Mr Hardcastle and the second to Mrs
Hardcastle. Each of the two characters is given a set of attitudes and
values: Mr Hardcastle is conservative, Mrs Hardcastle all for change.
Because this is a comedy, the conflict is often directed to humour, and
never life-threatening as it would be in tragedy, but nonetheless there
are important values which are being set up in opposition to each
other.

The most important question is not so much about the characters' attitudes, but the author's and then the audience's. To what
extent are we invited to take sides in the battle between the two
fictional characters, and ultimately, even if we recognise what the
author is up to, are we prepared to go along with it?

The play starts in the middle of a conversation, and although
Mrs Hardcastle has the first word, it is in reply to something said as
they enter. While Mrs Hardcastle talks about specific things, Mr
Hardcastle tends to moralise. This does not necessarily make him
more admirable, but it does suggest his views are more weighty. We
know that he too can be trivial – his old stories of battles – but we
don't hear him so. In terms of characterisation, then, Goldsmith gives
an immediate sense that the man is serious and the woman trivial.

Mrs Hardcastle also has qualities that are stereotypically female. While Mr Hardcastle is prepared to talk about his age, Mrs Hardcastle lies about hers (and is easily found out). While he sees the reality of Tony's behaviour, she is a doting mother who cannot see the obvious even when faced with it. And she is faced with it, which means that so are we the audience. The dramatic timing of first hearing Tony 'hal-looing' is comic, but it also makes it clear that she is indulgent and blind to her son's follies. The fact that Tony then ignores her affection as he pursues his own pleasure heightens the effect.

There are a number of ways an audience can respond to Mr Hardcastle, far fewer to Mrs Hardcastle. How Mr Hardcastle is seen will depend in part upon the performance of the actor; does he play Hardcastle as kindly and world-weary, or is he played with more severity? Although Mrs Hardcastle's values are belittled, this does not mean that Mr Hardcastle's are affirmed. After all, it would seem that he is as fixed in his views as his wife, prone to telling the same old stories, maybe even a bit vain in his way. But for all that, from this brief extract it would appear that the audience have been moved towards Mr Hardcastle as upholding the better set of values. This is not an absolute position though, and, as is the case with the best plays, there is scope for uncertainty. An interesting challenge for an actress would be to make Mrs Hardcastle an object of sympathy rather than humour.

Drama texts contain characters displaying certain attitudes and values and part of the impact of the play comes from the way the writer has shaped the play, encouraging the audience to respond to characters in certain ways.

The following dramatic techniques were identified in the discussion of *She Stoops to Conquer* as ways in which playwrights can encourage an audience's response:

◎ Naming systems and the connotations which go with names;
◎ Stereotypical behaviour of a group, gender etc.;
◎ The content of what characters say, expressed through the language they use; in this case if it is overstated or weak in argument, then the audience is less likely to accept it.
◎ Dramatic counterpointing between words and action, i.e. Mrs Hardcastle says Tony is weak, followed by us seeing the opposite.
◎ Seeing things happen **on** stage and having reports of things happening **off** it.

Additionally, if you read the whole play, you will find that much of its effect on the audience depends upon:

◎   confusion of place and identity, with the audience always in the most superior position because they see and so know more than the individual characters.

Conclusion

This chapter has looked specifically at drama, and some of the issues involved for English students when studying texts from this genre. The sheer impossibility of saying that there is one definitive version of a play, if we take the word 'version' to mean performance rather than written text, means that ambiguity and multiple readings are always going to be a feature of studying drama.

Within the discussion of drama in this chapter, a number of issues have been raised. At the forefront of the discussion have been ideas about drama, including:

◎   the historical context of the plays;
◎   comparison of different types of play;
◎   how scenes are staged including different ways of playing a scene to bring out different interpretations;
◎   the role of the audience in the dramatic presentation as a whole;
◎   characterisation, or the way a writer develops a role;
◎   the discussion of themes, of ideas in a play, by looking at what the writer does, and different ways of interpreting or playing the text;
◎   a review of a performance with a focus on a particular scene, 'problem' etc.;
◎   analysis of the way the playwright has shaped possible performances through stage directions, dramatic structure etc.;
◎   analysis of an important scene, seeing how it fits into the dramatic whole;
◎   features of the language in the play and how characters are created through the way they speak.

The context frame which is being applied throughout this book has been applied in the following ways. In terms of **the writer's context**, there are issues to explore concerning views held at the time when the text was written. In *She Stoops to Conquer*, there are contrasting perceptions of the town and the country, and these perceptions are rooted in differing political attitudes. Some of these issues remain relevant today, especially in debates over hunting and the place of the countryside in an essentially industrial society. So as far as **the reader's context** is concerned, how you respond to the argument between the Hardcastles may well depend on how you view contemporary differences between urban and rural perceptions.

The text's context for *She Stoops to Conquer* is partly governed by the fact that the play has remained popular, but is usually seen as a comedy of manners rather than a play with profound ideological significance. For *The Tempest*, on the other hand, there is a traditional view that because this is one of Shakespeare's later plays, it is about resolution and reconciliation, a playwright bringing down the curtain on his own career. While this may appeal to literary critics, it does not necessarily apply to an audience watching the play in the theatre.

The readings context has been explored through the idea that each performance of a play is in some way unique, which suggests that plays sustain multiple readings and that the audience will find the play potentially ambiguous in its meaning.

The language context has been explored in all the extracts through the way dramatic dialogue is managed by the playwright to influence audience reaction.

This chapter has looked at various issues surrounding the study of plays within a literature course. It has deliberately included extracts from Shakespeare plays to stress the point that they must be seen as works of drama. But, as has been noted earlier, Shakespeare is given a place all to himself in most courses, so the following chapter does the same, looking at one play in particular from a variety of different angles.

Chapter *seven*

Contexts and Shakespeare

No writer in English is more surrounded by attitudes and values than Shakespeare. It is probably impossible to hear his name without being influenced by all the many and varied associations which the playwright and his work evoke. He is the one writer all school pupils in England and Wales must now study. In many ways, he is the cornerstone of the **literary heritage** which to some people is an essential part of the subject English and the idea of 'Englishness'. In other words, his significance is political as well as literary.

Because Shakespeare is seen by many as a writer different from all other writers, it is perhaps to be expected that some strange things are written about him. Nonetheless, we should guard against falling into too easy an attitude, where because we are talking or writing about Shakespeare, we are not allowed to be honestly critical. Writing in the *Independent on Sunday* about recent films of Shakespeare's plays, Robert Butler said:

> These films are getting Shakespeare across to new audiences … Anyone who has struggled with a complicated Shakespearean plot or unfamiliar Elizabethan language will leap at the chance to see actors bring the story and characters alive.
>
> (*Independent on Sunday*, 13 February 2000)

There are at least two assertions to note here, both of which tend to be made about Shakespeare. The first is that while many people find Shakespeare difficult, for various reasons, these same people nonetheless want to see his plays. The evidence for this is hard to find. Just because films of Shakespeare's plays win awards and achieve reasonable viewing figures in art house cinemas, does not mean that the whole nation will 'leap at the chance' to view them. This myth of Shakespeare's supposed mass popularity is part of the same process which sees him as representing Englishness.

The second myth which at least needs to be questioned is that Shakespeare's characters 'come alive'. However well-drawn they may be, Shakespeare's characters, like all fictional creations, are representations of real life, not real life itself.

So, one result of the great significance accorded to Shakespeare is the difficulty for a student of responding to his writing without being weighed down by his reputation. Remember, though, that you are studying a play or plays, and that drama has its own conventions and contexts. Shakespeare wrote for the theatre, with a keen awareness of dramatic effects. It is important not to be overawed by the reputation and so lose sight of the theatricality of the plays. It is also important to focus on the various contexts of his plays, just as you would with any other writer.

One play, *The Taming of the Shrew*, will be used in this chapter to serve as an example of a number of aspects worth considering when studying a Shakespeare play. The general points that are made, within the 'context framework' of this book, will be applicable to other plays that you may study.

Shakespeare's *The Taming of the Shrew* was written early in his career, probably between 1590 and 1594. The following is a summary of the play's plot:

The play opens with a two-scene Induction in which a drunken rustic, Christopher Sly, is tricked by a Lord who finds him drunkenly asleep. The Lord tricks Sly into thinking that Sly is a lord who has been out of his mind for years, and has just returned to his senses. He is given rich clothes, food and wine and provided with a 'wife', the Lord's page, and is then entertained by watching a play performed. The play is *The Taming of the Shrew*. In other words, the main play is in fact a play-within-a-play.

Baptista of Padua has two daughters, Katharina and Bianca. Bianca has many suitors, but her father will not consent to her marrying anyone until her elder sister Katharina is married. Katharina has the reputation of a 'shrew': a noisy and 'froward' woman who is not biddable and docile like her younger sister. Petruchio, who wishes to find a wealthy wife, meets and marries Katharina. He 'tames' her into becoming a 'household conformable Kate' and the play ends with Katharina delivering a long speech in which she argues that women must obey their husbands in every way.

The writer's context – women, power and silence

There are, broadly speaking, three ways in which the writer's context can be approached; one is to consider where the text fits in terms of the writer's own life-story (if much is known about it); the second is to consider how one text relates to other works by the author; the third is to consider some of the political, social and cultural aspects of the time in which the text is written, and how these may have affected the writer's work.

Little is known about Shakespeare's life, although that has not stopped many 'biographers' and film-makers from making up a life for him. Although scholars attempt to date Shakespeare's plays, these are not always very precise either.

Rather more is known about social attitudes of his day. At the time of the first performance of the play, single women (unmarried or widowed) could:

◎   inherit and administer land;
◎   make a will;
◎   sign a contract;
◎   possess property;
◎   sue and be sued.

Married women could do none of these things.

In sixteenth- and seventeenth-century writings, marriage was commonly seen in terms of a political model, where a husband ruled over a wife like a king ruled over a State. She should submit to his rule and domination. Women were discouraged by strong social disapproval and physical punishment from speaking their minds freely and openly, not just in public debate but in private conversation. The 'shrew' was not just a figure of fun, but seen as a threat to public order, and physical punishment and humiliation was one remedy.

The origin of the word 'shrew' is worth noting here. Although literally 'a small creature', a shrew was also used to refer to something 'evil' or 'cursed'. The word 'shrewd' meant evil in nature, before its meaning gradually shifted to cunning, and then finally towards a more positive connotation of cleverness and skill.

103

In *The Taming of the Shrew*, the seemingly modest and quiet Bianca is clearly the favourite of her father, and the one who has several suitors; her shrewish (or shrewd) older sister cannot find anyone to marry her except Petruchio, who welcomes the chance to 'tame' her and make her into the kind of wife apparently thought desirable. He is also motivated by money. Bianca says about her sister after the wedding, that 'Being mad herself, she's madly mated'. It seems that Katharina cannot hope to find the sort of husband that other women might. Yet her marriage means that she becomes in a sense the 'property' of her husband. Just after the wedding, Petruchio says:

> I will be master of what is mine own.
> She is my goods, my chattels; she is my house,
> My household stuff, my field, my barn,
> My horse, my ox, my ass, my anything;
> And here she stands, touch her whoever dare.

Katharina then has no choice but to accompany Petruchio to his house and leave her home. The wedding itself seems designed to humiliate her, with Petruchio being late, turning up wearing bizarrely inappropriate clothing and behaving boorishly at the actual ceremony.

There are times during the play when the audience would expect Katharina, notorious previously for her forwardness and noise, to protest loudly. Yet sometimes she does not speak. The use of silences in drama can be powerful. A character on stage who doesn't speak is nonetheless saying something through their silence – just because they are not speaking does not mean that the audience is not watching them. In this play, there are crucial moments when Katharina does not speak, in spite of the fact that she is held up to ridicule. It is also noticeable that, unlike most of Shakespeare's more important female characters, particularly in the comedies, she has no female friend in whom to confide. Think about the plays of Shakespeare familiar to you and whether the female characters are isolated in this way. It is not easy to think of one, except perhaps Ophelia in *Hamlet*, and madness and death are her fate.

As Katharina has no female friend to consult, and as there are times when the play silences her, her vulnerability is emphasised. This makes it hard for a modern audience, with very different values about men and women, to accept her 'taming' at the hands of her husband. The power seems too unequally divided.

One example of Katharina's silence occurs after she has met Petruchio for the first time. They talk in what we might think of as a sparky way, and it seems that the playwright might be suggesting an attraction between them. But when the two of them are joined by her father, Baptista, and two other male characters, Katharina has little to say. She refers to Petruchio as 'a madcap ruffian and a swearing jack' and suggests that her father cannot really love her if he wishes to marry her off to him. When Petruchio says he intends to wed her on Sunday, she replies 'I'll see thee hanged on Sunday first'.

After this, there are about thirty lines before her exit, but none of them is spoken by Katharina, even though she is on stage to hear Petruchio blatantly lie about her previous actions, and he goes on to plan the wedding with her father. Katharina's behaviour on stage here is a challenge for both director and actor. What does she do while this is going on?

The fact that this is a female character is significant. We are caught up in issues of **power** here. Katharina has considerably less choice than many of the male characters. Four hundred years after the first performances of these plays, the interpretation of female silences by actors and audiences will inevitably be different from earlier performances, since we bring an entirely different awareness of gender roles and choices to the plays.

A further example of the treatment of women in the play *The Taming of the Shrew* occurs in Act 2, scene 1. Since Katharina is now to be married, her younger sister is available for marriage too. Baptista appears to 'auction' his daughter Bianca to the highest bidder as he addresses two suitors:

Content you, gentlemen, I will compound this strife.
'Tis deeds must win the prize, and he of both
That can assure my daughter greatest dower
Shall have my Bianca's love.

You can see here that Baptista combines legal and financial language ('compound', 'deeds', 'prize') with 'love'. He also assumes that his daughter's 'love' is in his possession, and can be given away by him. Bianca, like Katharina and many other female characters in Shakespeare's plays, has limited choices.

In other words, at the points at which modern drama might begin to bite – think about the way soap opera handles relationships – the plot begins to focus on another aspect or idea. In the same way, any moral misgivings we might have about Petruchio's methods of 'taming' his wife in the way that a wild creature might be tamed, by hunger and sleeplessness, must be overlooked if we are to find the play a 'comedy'. Yet in our context, not just the methods, but the whole concept of changing a woman by force into a meeker and milder creature, are deeply suspect.

What all this means is that we cannot simply accept a Shakespeare play as something unproblematic, just because it was written by this cornerstone of our literary heritage.

Task

1   In the Shakespeare play or plays you are studying, consider the dramatic role of a character who could be seen as a confidante. Think in particular how such characters allow Shakespeare to present to an audience the thoughts and feelings of a main character.

2   In the Shakespeare play or plays you are studying, see if there is a scene where a marriage is proposed, organised or looked back upon. How is the woman's role in the marriage presented by Shakespeare?

3   In the Shakespeare play or plays you are studying, find a scene where a character is on stage for some time but is silent. Consider some of the issues concerning the staging of this scene and then try to match your own ideas with those in a genuine production. If this is not possible, watch a version or versions on video. Do the film directors, for instance, dodge the issue of silence by keeping the character off-camera?

The text's context – versions and sources

One commonly-held view of so-called 'great' writers is that they are the originators of wonderful plots and stories. This is certainly not the case with Shakespeare, who used many different sources for his plays. It is what he did with those sources which is worth studying.

In the case of *The Taming of the Shrew*, events of the plot of Bianca and her suitors come directly from Gascoigne's *Supposes* (1566) which is an adaptation of Ariosto's *I Suppositi*. The source for the Petruchio/Katharina relationship is a folk-tale about taming a difficult wife. There were many versions of this circulating in England at this time, and these included ballads (e.g. 'A Merry Jest of a Shrewd and Curst Wife Lapped in Morel's Skin for her Good Behaviour').

It is easy to assume that the text you are using when studying a play by Shakespeare is the only version. In fact, fewer than half of Shakespeare's plays were published in his lifetime. The plays would have been written for the company he worked for and, after censoring, turned into 'prompt books' which were used for the production. Individual actors received only copies of their own lines and cues. Therefore, the play was seen only in actual performance, and would still have been changed. During Shakespeare's lifetime, nearly half of his plays were published as 'quartos' – in effect pirated versions of the plays, perhaps memorised by actors, or written in shorthand by members of the audience.

Shakespeare died in 1616, and in 1623, his plays were collected by two fellow actors, John Heminge and Henry Condell, in an edition known as the 'First Folio'. There are sometimes big differences between the Quarto and Folio versions. (The words quarto and folio refer to the size of the original formats). These differences are so large in some cases (particularly *King Lear*) that they might be considered as two separate texts. As far as *The Taming of the Shrew* is concerned, there is evidence that it was performed as early as 1594, almost thirty years before the publication of the text. But the First Folio is the only version now available. There might have been many changes during that time. The situation is further complicated by the existence of another similar play (see below for further discussion of this).

It is important to contextualise the production of a text, with an awareness and an examination of our own attitudes to authorship. We have different assumptions today about what constitutes a 'text', and different views on the concept of 'originality'. It would be wrong to think that Shakespeare was anything other than a working playwright, which means that his plays do not exist in a single somehow perfect version.

Task

1 If you are studying Shakespeare for coursework, one possible task would be to see what use he makes of his sources. Certain editions of his plays, available in libraries, give lengthy appendices which include source material: the Arden, Riverside or Norton editions are good starting points. There are at least two possible areas you could focus on: how Shakespeare both uses and adapts the original plots; and how he both uses and adapts the original language.

2   As an example of different texts, compare these two versions of *King Lear*. Quarto 1 was first printed in 1607–8, whilst Folio 1 appeared in 1623. It is possible that the Quarto is the play written by Shakespeare, as yet not performed, whilst Folio 1 is the revised version, produced after the play was performed. The editors of the most recent Oxford editions of the plays (1986) choose to see them as two separate texts, each with its own integrity. Most other editors produce a 'conflated' version of the two.

King Lear, in his old age, has decided to divide his kingdom up amongst his three daughters.

Act 1 scene 1
Meantime we will express our darker purposes.
The map there. Know we have divided
In three our kingdom, and 'tis our first intent
To shake all cares and business off our state,
Confirming them on younger years.

Act 1 scene 1
Meantime we shall express our darker purpose.
Give me the map there. Know that we have divided
In three our kingdom, and 'tis our fast intent
To shake all cares and business from our age,
Conferring them on younger strengths while we
Unburdened crawl towards death.

3   In the Shakespeare play or plays you are studying, try to find scenes where differences between versions are pronounced and work out the varying impact of each version. This could form part of a coursework submission, for example.

The play *The Taming of the Shrew* has its own textual complications. A play called *The Taming of a Shrew* was published in a quarto edition in 1594 and reprinted in 1596 and 1607. *The Taming of the Shrew* was first published in 1623 (the First Folio). The attitude that Shakespeare's text (however problematic) is untouchable and somehow sacred is relatively modern. Earlier approaches were less reverent: John Fletcher wrote a sequel to the play in 1611 called *The Woman's Prize, or The Tamer Tamed*. The actor David Garrick wrote an adaptation of the play called *Catharine and Petruchio* in the eighteenth century, and between 1754 and 1844 that was the only version performed on stage in England and America.

The relationship between the two plays *A Shrew* and *The Shrew* is problematic. It has been thought that Shakespeare used *A Shrew* as a source, or that it was an unauthorised version of *The Shrew*, reconstructed from actors' memories. Another alternative is that both plays are versions of an older play, now lost. One approach is to regard them as two separate texts, each with its own strengths and weaknesses. In one respect, *A Shrew* is more sophisticated, in that the Induction framework is completed. In *The Shrew*, the characters of the Induction make only one further brief appearance within the play, whilst in *A Shrew* they conclude the play as well.

Task

The final speech of Katharina in *The Taming of the Shrew* has a great deal of dramatic emphasis placed on it. It is unusually long, and delivered to most of the characters in the play, as well as to the audience. Apart from a few final lines, it concludes the play. It is also very problematic for a modern audience because, taken at face value, it suggests that women should be totally submissive to their husbands. This means that actors and directors have to find a way of playing this scene in such a way that it will work within the context of modern attitudes towards social roles of men and women.

There are significant differences, however, between the speech in *The Taming of the Shrew* (page 111) and the speech in *The Taming of A Shrew* (page 110). How is the main focus of each speech different?

Commentary

In the first play, Katharina compares the roles of husband and wife to prince and subject. She claims that men and women inhabit different spheres of life for which their physical strength best equips them. In the second, the argument is religious: women are more sinful and therefore morally inferior. They are responsible for the fall of humanity, and they should therefore submit to men's will. The version we currently know as Shakespeare's is clearly contributing to a debate about the social position and status of women, whereas the second version, whose authorship is uncertain, explains women's position in terms of the Old Testament and religious convention. Does this mean that even when these plays were written, the argument that women should obey their husbands was not as clear-cut as may seem to be the case if we only look at one version of the play?

Text   *The Taming of the Shrew*

A woman moved is like a fountain troubled,
Muddy, ill-seeming, thick, bereft of beauty;
And while it is so, none so dry or thirsty
Will deign to sip or touch one drop of it.
Thy husband is thy lord, thy life and thy keeper,
Thy head, thy sovereign; one that cares for thee,
And for thy maintenance commits his body
To painful labour both by sea and land,
To watch the night in storms, the day in cold,
Whilst thou liest warm at home, secure and safe;
And craves no other tribute at thy hands
But love, fair looks and true obedience
Too little payment for so great a debt.
Such duty as the subject owes the prince,
Even such a woman oweth to her husband;
And when she is froward, peevish, sullen, sour
And not obedient to his honest will,
What is she but a foul contending rebel
And graceless traitor to her loving lord?
I am ashamed that women are so simple
To offer war where they should kneel for peace,
Or seek for rule, supremacy, and sway,
When they are bound to serve, love and obey.
Why are our bodies soft, and weak, and smooth,
Unapt to toil and trouble in the world,
But that our soft conditions and our hearts
Should well agree with our external parts?
Come. Come, you froward and unable worms!
My mind hath been as big as one of yours,
My heart as great, my reason haply more,
To bandy word for word and frown for frown;
But now I see our lances are but straws,
Our strength as weak, our weakness past compare,
That seeming to be most which we indeed least are.
Then vail your stomachs, for it is no boot,
And place your hands below your husband's foot,
In token of which duty, if he please,
My hand is ready; may it do him ease.

Text   *The Taming of a Shrew*

Then you that live thus by your pampered wills,
Now list to me and mark what I shall say.
Th'eternal power that with His only breath,
Shall cause this end and this beginning frame,
Not in time, nor before time, but with time, confused;
For all the course of years, of ages, months,
Of seasons temperate, of days and hours,
Are tuned and stopped by labour of His hand.
The first world was a form without a form,
A heap confused, a mixture all deformed,
A gulf of gulfs, a body bodiless,
Where all the elements were orderless,
Before the great commander of the world,
The King of Kings, the glorious God of Heaven,
Who in six days did frame His heavenly work,
And made all things to stand in perfect course.
Then to His image he did make a man,
Old Adam; and from his side asleep,
A rib was taken, of which the Lord did make
The woe of man, so termed by Adam then
Woman, for that by her came sin to us,
And for her sin was Adam doomed to die.
As Sarah to her husband, so should we
Obey them, love them, keep and nourish them,
If they by any means do want our helps,
Laying our hands under their feet to tread,
If that by that we might procure their ease.
And for a precedent I'll first begin,
And lay my hand under my husband's feet.

[*She lays her hand under her husband's feet.*]

Fie, fie! Unknit that threatening unkind brow,
And dart not scornful glances from those eyes
To wound thy lord, thy king, thy governor.
It bolts thy beauty as frosts do bite the meads,
Confounds thy fame as whirlwinds shake fair buds,
And in no sense is meet or amiable.

Reader's context/readings context – identity and social roles

Katharina's final speech involves the idea of social roles and identity. Some interpretations of the play are based on the way in which Petruchio 'releases' Kate from the role she has become trapped in of shrew. However, a modern audience might take issue with the assumption that he has the right to determine what her role should be. It may seem that he enjoys the power which he is given over Kate: a power he has by virtue of being male and prepared to marry her. At one stage in the play (Act IV, scene 3) Kate is allowed to return to her father's home only if she accepts his view of reality. She has to accept that he can define the time of day, even when he is clearly lying.

Petruchio says:

Look what I speak, or do, or think to do,
You are still crossing it.

To be obedient she must even try to work out what he is thinking!

In her last speech (quoted above) she focuses on the relative roles of men and women. It is certainly true that in this play, there is an emphasis on the roles of women in society, and a clear indication that the ideal woman is quiet and biddable. Petruchio declares his aim to make Kate 'conformable, household Kate' even though he is initially attracted to and challenged by her spirit. A modern audience may well question whether Kate can really be presented to us as happier when she has ceased to fight against her role in life.

A recent American production with an all-female cast provoked very different responses to the issues in the play. In Shakespeare's time, however, the play would have been performed by an all-male cast, which would again have affected how an audience viewed what happened to Kate.

It is crucial to remember that Shakespeare's texts are plays, and that they are meant to be performed. The genre of a text cannot be ignored. You should watch productions of the plays you are studying if you possibly can. It is also important for you to bear in mind that every performance is an interpretation. There can be no definitive production. Even if you don't agree with particular decisions about a production of the play, it is still useful to analyse what it is that you don't like, and why.

As far as *The Taming of the Shrew* is concerned, there are particular problems for modern productions. A modern audience may well object to the concept and methods of the 'taming'. It is not possible to 'unlearn' present-day experiences and attitudes. Therefore directors of the play have to decide what to do about the arguably misogynistic nature of the play. Katharina's long final speech is a crucial test of how attitudes in the play are presented.

Reference has already been made to the easily available BBC version (1980). The casting of John Cleese in the part of Petruchio suggests that the comedy in the play will be a foregone conclusion: John Cleese inevitably brings with him the associations of the television roles for which he is famous. The director, Jonathan Miller, revealingly referred to Petruchio's task in the taming of Kate as 'bringing a spirited steed under control'.

The casting of the two main parts is also significant. One famous film version, still available on video, cast Elizabeth Taylor and Richard Burton as Kate and Petruchio, with all the connotations of two famous stars involved in their own tumultuous relationship. In another version, the stars of the television series 'Moonlighting', Bruce Willis and Cybill Shepherd, acted the two parts, although here their version did not end with a speech of capitulation by Kate. This version included a framing device of a boy whose mother would not let him watch 'Moonlighting'. Instead he starts reading a copy of *The Taming of the Shrew*. Here the play ends with Kate's refusal to accept her husband's view of reality: he has to agree with her.

The 1999 American film *10 Things I Hate about You* is another adaptation of the play, as is Cole Porter's musical *Kiss me Kate*. Each version of the play in some way reflects the fact that the time when it was produced has affected the interpretation offered.

Kate's speech, quoted in its entirety above, presents particular problems of interpretation, and so is especially worth looking at in various performances. In this case, does the actor playing Kate deliver this speech ironically or not? She is actually telling other women to acknowledge the rightful authority of their husbands, and doing this to prove her husband right in order for him to win a bet he has made with other men. Some productions will emphasise her complicity, as if there is a secret understanding between her and Petruchio. Yet to do this is to ignore the process of taming she has had to suffer, based on withholding food and sleep, and forcing her to accept Petruchio's view of reality. Other productions might stress the fact that she has in a way been brainwashed by her treatment, retaining little of her own identity. The delivery of this speech is a key to the interpretation of the whole play.

The RSC touring version of 2000 played Kate's final speech very 'straight'. The audience watching were initially bemused. How could the play end on such a note? All became clear, though, when the play did not end with this speech, but with a return to Sly. His mockery by the women at the disco made the audience realise that his male fantasy was not matched by reality; men like Sly might like to think they can tame women, but they can't really.

Task

Similar key moments to the one identified above can be found in other plays. Make a detailed study of how different actors and directors have approached such scenes in a play or plays you are studying.

The language context – induction as framing device

One strand of **the language context** framework introduced in Chapter 1 asks: How is the text's narrative organised?

The Taming of the Shrew is introduced by an Induction which lasts two scenes. In the Induction, Christopher Sly, 'a tinker and beggar', a drunken English rustic and therefore to be seen as comical, is discovered lying dead drunk by a Lord returning from hunting. Then there begins a joke at Sly's expense, in which he is persuaded that he himself is in fact a wealthy lord who has lost his wits, and has now returned to his proper identity. There is much humour at Sly's expense. The Lord refers to the drunkenly sleeping Sly at first sight as a 'monstrous beast' and 'like a swine' but decides he will 'practice on this drunken man'. Sly is treated as if he were a lord, bestowed with clothing, furnishings, food and drink all suitable for his new status. The bewildered Sly asks:

Am I a lord? And have I such a lady?
Or do I dream? Or have I dreamed till now?

A page is dressed up as a woman, and presented to Sly as his 'wife'. Sly eagerly says:

Servants, leave me and her alone.
Madam, undress you and come you now to bed.

But the Lord has arranged delaying tactics: players who are to perform a play for this 'Lord'. And the play is *The Taming of the Shrew* which immediately becomes a play-within-a-play.

A number of issues are raised by The Induction: for example, what constitutes identity; what we say we are; what others think we are; how we behave; how others treat us; the language we use? In George Bernard Shaw's play *Pygmalion* the flower-girl Eliza Doolittle is transformed into a society woman, at least superficially, by changing the way she speaks and acts. One of Shaw's ideas in the play is the way that language can appear to construct an identity. Another idea is the responsibility of one who undertakes such a transformation; are they really changing someone for the 'better' or interfering in human lives? In *The Taming of the Shrew* the issue of responsibility is not dealt with: the comedy is at Sly's expense and nobody is expected to question it.

Katharina too is seemingly transformed from a shrew into an obedient wife, but the issues about identity raised by the Induction will also apply here. Is she really changed? Does any one person have the right to set out deliberately to change another, either for fun, for money, or even seemingly for their own good? Can we make those decisions on behalf of someone else? If we do, are we dehumanising them?

The Induction, therefore, introduces ideas which are important in the play. But it serves other functions too. It frames the 'real' play and therefore distances it. In one sense this means that the play is removed from much of the criticism we might want to make; it is, after all, not a 'real' play, but one put on for a drunken fool. He is not a sophisticated audience, so we cannot expect a sophisticated play. This idea can be heightened by having Sly on stage throughout the performance; yet another variable dependent on how a director approaches the task.

The distancing is reflected in the play in other ways too. For example, when the audience first sees Katharina, Baptista, and Bianca and her suitors, we see them in a way through the eyes of the character Lucentio and his servant Tranio, the first characters we meet after the Induction. They are the ones who observe what Tranio refers to as 'some show to welcome us to town'. So they watch the 'show', watched by Sly and his 'wife'. And they in turn are watched by the audience.

The BBC version of the play, with John Cleese as Petruchio, dispenses with the Induction altogether. Most recent productions include it, though, with the RSC 2000 version going a step further by returning to the Induction with a scene of its own invention. Sly wakes up after his 'wonderful dream' and decides he will go and chat up women in the local disco. At once he is rebuffed, and the play ends with Sly being ridiculed for his inability to talk to women.

The Taming of a Shrew also ends by returning to the characters of the Induction. In this version, Sly is returned to his old clothes and environment. He says 'Am I not a Lord?' and decides all that has happened was a dream, though the dream has shown him how 'to tame a shrew'. It was the best dream he has ever had in his life, and he intends to go to his wife 'and tame her too'.

By seeing the whole play within the play as a 'dream' – which happens in both versions mentioned above – doubt is cast on the whole process of taming. Since Sly, a comical and drunken character, intends to 'tame' his wife, the audience will be left with doubts about the whole idea of 'taming': in effect, Sly undermines it and suggests it is potentially laughable. Questions are raised about identity: how easy is it to assume and discard roles in society? Does the way we are treated affect the person we become?

The Induction, then, can have considerable impact on how we read the rest of the play, *The Taming of the Shrew*. Possible issues include: anticipating questions about identity; looking at ideas about change and transformation; making acceptable some unpleasant attitudes and behaviour.

Task

Although other Shakespeare plays do not have such an unusual narrative device as a half-finished Induction, many contain a sub-plot which in some way casts light on the main action. In a play or plays you are studying, analyse how the sub-plot is used by Shakespeare to create dramatic interest and contrast.

Conclusion

This chapter has looked at a Shakespeare play, *The Taming of the Shrew*, from a number of viewpoints. It has been used as an example which can be followed for the study of other plays. Discussion of social attitudes in Shakespeare's time are part of **the writer's context**; so is the discussion of the idea of women and silence in the sixteenth century.

In looking at notions of women and power, and comparing the sixteenth century with modern times, we are approaching the play from **the reader's context**. The same goes for discussing identity and social roles in the play.

Various versions of the text, sources for the play and different productions are all part of **the text's context**. The role of the Induction, and its inclusion or otherwise in the play, are partly to do with **the text's context**, and partly to do with **the language context**, as whether or not the Induction is included has a considerable impact on the narrative of the play and how its story is told.

All of the above work on this play leads to discussions on issues such as what constitutes identity, how we respond to Kate's final speech, what meanings the play offers. **The readings context** encompasses how a play is ultimately interpreted, both by an actor and director who 'produce' the play, and the audience who receive it. This audience is not one homogeneous group, though; very different attitudes and assumptions will be held by a theatre full of viewers.

Chapter eight

Similarity and difference

Throughout this book it has been argued that texts do not appear suddenly from nowhere; they must be placed within a context. This chapter will explore some issues around the idea that texts can often be read and understood by reference to other texts. Using the context frame in Chapter 1, this means focusing in particular on **the text's context**, and looking at some of the issues raised by the question: what is the text's relationship to other texts?

Intertextuality

In one sense it can be argued that everything you read as an individual must be affected by what you have read before; this is the way your reading skills improve. The same argument can be made for larger cultural groups; the way we read a text collectively is affected by the way our culture has read other texts in the past. So, for example, if we read a children's fable, the way we understand that fable will be conditioned by a number of things that we have already discovered from reading other fables. These might include:

◎ fables have a particular form and use a certain sort of language;
◎ fables have animals that represent people;
◎ fables end with a moral.

It can also be argued that all literary works which belong recognisably to a certain genre of writing are intertextual in that the reader brings to them certain expectations, and the writer operates within certain parameters. Texts labelled as 'Crime', 'Romance', 'Science Fiction', 'Horror' etc. refer implicitly to other texts in the same genre, and often explicitly too (for a fuller discussion of genre see below).

In a broad sense, then, everything we read is understood through what we have read before, but this chapter will focus in particular on the ways that literary texts make reference to other literary texts. This process is called **intertextuality**.

There are many ways in which literary texts make specific reference to other texts.

1   An obvious way is through the title of a work. Dylan Thomas wrote a book called *Portrait of the Artist as a Young Dog*, echoing James Joyce's *Portrait of the Artist as a Young Man*. As might be expected, many titles use Shakespearean quotations: H.E. Bates's novel *The Darling Buds of May* quotes from *Sonnet 18* (see below); Thomas Hardy's *Under the Greenwood Tree* from *As You Like It*; Aldous Huxley's *Brave New World* from *The Tempest*. Hardy also quotes, this time from Gray's *Elegy*, in his title *Far From the Madding Crowd*. Using in a title **allusions** from other works does not necessarily mean that the new work is based wholly or even partly upon the old, but it does suggest that the author is alerting the reader to a shared point of reference – provided, that is, the reader is aware of the allusion in the first place.

2   Another way authors can use allusions is to place them within the substance of their own text, rather than just with a title. Poetry is a particularly suitable medium for this; it is read more closely than prose and is often more opaque in its meaning. A good example of this process is in T.S. Eliot's *The Waste Land*, a poem which makes little accommodation for those who do not recognise the allusions and with which many students struggle unless they read the poem with an accompanying guide.

3   There is more to intertextuality than allusion, however. Myths and legends, for example, are frequently re-worked by authors wishing to give a new gloss to an old story. George Bernard Shaw's play *Pygmalion* takes a Greek legend and echoes many of its ideas in the story of Henry Higgins and Eliza Doolittle.

4   **Parody** involves reference to other texts, this time as much to do with form and language as with plot and ideas. Some parody

imitates for comic purposes; other parody, such as Pope's *Rape of the Lock,* imitates classical epic poetry but at the same time makes serious points of its own. *Sonnet 130* by Shakespeare (see below) is another example.

5   **Genre transformation** is another way intertextuality can work. Genre transformation involves taking a text, say a novel, and re-working it in another genre, say a television adaptation. *My Fair Lady* is a musical based on *Pygmalion*, and *Kiss Me Kate* is a musical based on *The Taming of the Shrew*, using a quotation from the original as the title of the new work. The film *Apocalypse Now* was loosely based on Conrad's novel *Heart of Darkness*, which has itself been seen by critics as reflecting archetypal myths ranging from the Bible, Virgil and Dante.

6   Twentieth-century literature has a number of examples of literary works in which writers do more than allude or imitate; they take a well-known text and re-present it, often by using a different narrative perspective than that found in the original. Jean Rhys' *Wide Sargasso Sea* looks at *Jane Eyre* from the perspective of the first Mrs Rochester. Tom Stoppard's play *Rosencrantz and Guildenstern Are Dead* takes two minor characters from *Hamlet* and puts them in the spotlight. Peter Carey's *Jack Maggs* takes Magwitch from *Great Expectations* and explores what 'happens' to him after he leaves the original novel (see below). In these examples, writers are both looking at the attitudes and values in the original texts and at the same time making new texts of their own.

Task

Try to find other examples of your own for some or all of the categories above.

William Shakespeare   *Sonnets 18, 130*

The following sonnets are by Shakespeare, being numbers 18 and 130 in a sequence of 154. In writing sonnets, Shakespeare was using a form that was very popular at the time, especially for writing love poems and/or poems in honour of a rich benefactor. A sonnet has fourteen lines, and usually some form of organisation within these lines. What is often called the Shakespearean sonnet divides the poem into twelve lines of alternate rhymes, followed by a **rhyming couplet**, which is **graphologically** highlighted by being indented. The twelve lines can be subdivided into various permutations of four; 3×4, $8 + 4$, $4 + 8$ etc. These permutations can reflect subdivisions of meaning and argument as well as technical issues such as rhyme.

Shakespeare was not just working within a well-known form; he was writing at a time when a particular use was made of this form. Sonnet writers were often professional flatterers, writing for money and in competition with each other. One way to make your mark was to produce striking **metaphors**, to use comparison as the form of flattery.

From this brief introduction it should be clear that there is already intertextuality at work here. Shakespeare is both using a traditional poetic form, the sonnet, and writing a sequence of sonnets which will in some way interact with each other. He is aware that the sonnets of his time were particularly reliant on metaphor, comparisons which would find new ways of saying much the same thing – that the person about whom the poem is written is in some way or another perfect.

Task

Read *Sonnet 18* at least twice. Then prepare notes on the following:

1   What is the main metaphor used here which gives the poem its overall impetus? How does Shakespeare undermine the metaphor even as he uses it?
2   What do you understand the final couplet to mean? You could consider here who are the various readers of the poem. Look again at the discussion of pronoun reference and Pope's epigram in Chapter 2 to help you here.

Text   *Sonnet 18*

Shall I compare thee to a summer's day?
Thou art more lovely and more temperate.
Rough winds do shake the darling buds of May,
And summer's lease hath all too short a date.
Sometime too hot the eye of heaven shines,
And often is his gold complexion dimmed;

And every fair from fair sometimes declines,
By chance, or nature's changing course, untrimmed;
But thy eternal summer shall not fade,
Nor lose possession of that fair thou ow'st,
Nor shall Death brag thou wand'rest in his shade,
When in eternal lines to time thou grow'st.
    So long as men can breathe or eyes can see
    So long lives this, and this gives life to thee.

Commentary

The main metaphor is signalled immediately by Shakespeare, and it is emphasised by being a single line that is **end-stopped**. It involves the comparison of the lover with a summer's day; except, of course, it doesn't, because although the metaphor is introduced to the reader (both lover and all other readers) it is given in a question form. Is this metaphor good enough? The question is soon answered because, by using the word 'more' in the next line, Shakespeare in effect says that the metaphor is inadequate. Although he continues to use it, at least up to line 9, he has given a new slant to a popular format; he has intertextually reflected other sonnets, but given a new angle on the process.

The final couplet also does something rather different than might be expected. Love poems which are addressed to the loved one, but which at the same time are published for all to read, are pretending to be private when they are in fact public. The pronoun 'thee' could be anyone, male or female, real or imaginary. But the pretence of this being personal rather than public is undermined by the demonstrative pronoun 'this' which comes in the last line. 'this' too is unreferenced, but as readers of the text, and being unable to access any possible private reference, we have to assume that 'this' is probably the poem itself. The couplet is not so much about the lover, but about the poem itself – and the 'I' who speaks the poem from the very start. It is 'I', who sees the weakness in the traditional metaphors of so many conventional love poems, who 'gives life' to 'thee'.

There are various ways we can react to this. Is Shakespeare, or his created voice, being self-congratulatory? Or is Shakespeare standing back from the voice which speaks the poem and saying that all that love poets really do is glorify themselves and show off? Both readings of the sonnet – and others too – are possible.

Now read *Sonnet 130*.

Text *Sonnet 130*

> My mistress' eyes are nothing like the sun;
> Coral is far more red than her lips red;
> If snow be white, why then her breasts are dun;
> If hairs be wires, black wires grow on her head.
> I have seen roses damasked, red and white,
> But no such roses see I in her cheeks,
> And in some perfumes is there more delight
> Than in the breath that from my mistress reeks.
> I love to hear her speak, yet well I know
> That music hath a far more pleasing sound.
> I grant I never saw a goddess go;
> My mistress when she walks treads on the ground.
>   And yet, by heaven, I think my love as rare,
>   As any she belied with false compare.

Task

1 Make a list of the lover's physical attributes which are placed for comparison, and alongside list the metaphors which Shakespeare rejects.
2 How does the final couplet take the poem in a new direction?
3 What similarities/differences can you find between this sonnet and *Sonnet 18*? Does *Sonnet 130* at any point seem to echo, intertextually, *Sonnet 18*?

Commentary

Your list will look something like this:

eyes	nothing like the sun
lips	not as red as coral
breasts	not white but dun (i.e. brown, dull)
hair(s)	if wires, then they are black wires
cheeks	not damasked (i.e. mixed) red and white
breath	not like perfume
voice	not like music
walk/weight	more substantial than a goddess

Shakespeare's narrative persona is here rejecting the types of similes and metaphors to be found in other poems, his own included. He is also commenting on the stereotypical representations of female beauty current at the time, some of which sound strange to modern readers. He is saying that people are people, not gods.

The final couplet has no metaphorical language, and although the speaker refers to heaven, he does so in an oath rather than a comparison. His beloved, he says, is as rare as anyone else's, indeed she is more so because she is not misrepresented by the type of false comparisons found in most poems.

Both sonnets look at the weakness of certain comparisons, both featuring the word 'compare' in the text. In *Sonnet 18* the metaphor is not strong enough, in *Sonnet 130* the metaphors are too strong and therefore far-fetched. The different way the word 'more' is used in each poem highlights this. There is, then, not only intertextuality at work in the way each poem reflects other unnamed poems, but also intertextual connection between these two poems. It can also be argued that the main intention of *Sonnet 130* is to raise a smile, rather than to be particularly serious.

The brief commentaries on these poems have focused on intertextuality. There are, however, many other ways they can be approached. *Sonnet 130* in particular can be read in a number of ways; with regard to its representation of gender for instance.

Task

The following poem called *Hekatompathia* is by Thomas Watson and was first published in 1581, before *Sonnet 130*. Its spelling has been modernised. What connections can you find between this poem and *Sonnet 130*? Note that no commentary follows this task.

Text *Hekatompathia*

Hark you that like to hear what saint I serve:
Her yellow locks exceed the beaten gold;
Her sparkling eyes in heaven a place deserve;
Her forehead high and fair of comely mould;
    Her words are music all of silver sound;
    Her wit so sharp as like as scarce be found:
Her eyebrow hangs like Iris in the skies
Her eagle's nose is straight of stately frame;
On either cheek a rose and lily lies;
Her breath is sweet perfume or holy flame;
    Her lips more red than any coral stone;
    Her neck more white that aged swans at mone;
Her breast transparent is, like crystal rock;
Her fingers long, fit for Apollo's lute;
Her slipper such as Momus dare not mock;
Her virtues all so great as make me mute:
    What other parts she hath I need not say,
    Whose face alone is cause of my decay.

Charles Dickens *Great Expectations*
Peter Carey *Jack Maggs*

This next section looks at an apparently obvious example of intertextuality. The contemporary Australian author Peter Carey takes one of the central strands from Dickens' *Great Expectations* and reworks it from a different perspective. Inevitably when dealing with intertextuality, some knowledge of the 'source' material is required.

Dickens' novel is narrated by the central character, Pip, who has an ambition to be a gentleman; he has great expectations. Early in the novel, when still a boy, he helps, albeit through fear, an escaped convict called Magwitch. Magwitch is eventually transported for life for unnamed crimes, but he remembers the help he received from the boy, and as he becomes wealthy in his new land, he secretly provides Pip with the finance that enables him to realise his ambition.

Against the terms of his transportation, Magwitch returns to England to see his protégé. Pip is at first repelled by him, but he hides him, and then takes care of him after he has been severely hurt in his

126

recapture. Pip sits by his bedside and contemplates what is happening to himself:

> and in the hunted wounded shackled creature who held my hand in his, I only saw a man who had meant to be my bene-factor ... only saw him a much better man than I.

At the end of the novel, Dickens suggests that although Pip loses all his money when Magwitch dies, he finally becomes a gentleman; not because he has money and status, but because he can feel for others.

Task – Great Expectations

The following extract comes near the end of the novel when Magwitch dies. Read it carefully at least twice, then make notes, ideally within a group, on the following questions.

1   Look at the dialect features of Magwitch's speech. How does Dickens place Magwitch in terms of social class through these? Then look at the way Magwitch uses metaphor in his speech. What might Dickens intend us to think about Magwitch?
2   The narrative at this point consists of a mixture of dialogue and commentary by Pip. Look closely at Pip's commentary, and consider what he has to say and how Dickens presents his comments.
3   A dictionary definition of the word 'sentimental' is 'excessive expression of feeling'. What features in this extract could be described as sentimental?

Text   Great Expectations

'Dear boy,' he said, as I sat down by his bed: 'I thought you was late. But I knowed you couldn't be that.'

'It is just the time,' said I. 'I waited for it at the gate.'

'You always waits at the gate; don't you, dear boy?'

'Yes. Not to lose a moment of the time.'

'Thank'ee dear boy, thank'ee. God bless you! You've never deserted me, dear boy.'

I pressed his hand in silence, for I could not forget that I had once meant to desert him.

'And what's the best of all,' he said, 'you've been more comfortable alonger me, since I was under a dark cloud, than when the sun shone. That's best of all.'

He lay on his back, breathing with great difficulty. Do what he would, and love me though he did, the light left his face ever and again, and a film came over the placid look at the white ceiling.

'Are you in much pain to-day?'

'I don't complain of none, dear boy.'

'You never do complain.'

He had spoken his last words. He smiled, and I understood his touch to mean that he wished to lift my hand, and lay it on his breast. I laid it there, and he smiled again, and put both his hands upon it.

The allotted time ran out, while we were thus; but, looking round, I found the governor of the prison standing near me, and he whispered, 'You needn't go yet.' I thanked him gratefully, and asked, 'Might I speak to him, if he can hear me?'

The governor stepped aside, and beckoned the officer away. The change, though it was made without noise, drew back the film from the placid look at the white ceiling, and he looked most affectionately at me.

'Dear Magwitch, I must tell you, now at last. You understand what I say?'

A gentle pressure on my hand.

'You had a child once, whom you loved and lost.'

A stronger pressure on my hand.

'She lived and found powerful friends. She is living now. She is a lady and very beautiful. And I love her!'

With a last faint effort, which would have been powerless but for my yielding to it and assisting it, he raised my hand to his lips. Then, he gently let it sink upon his breast again, with his own hands lying on it. The placid look at the white ceiling came back, and passed away, and his head dropped quietly on his breast.

Mindful, then, of what we had read together, I thought of the two men who went up into the Temple to pray, and I knew there were no better words that I could say beside his bed, than 'O Lord, be merciful to him, a sinner!'

Commentary

Magwitch's grammar is used to suggest a dialect form of English, although this dialect is not an authentic one such as cockney. Some features you may have spotted are as follows, (the grammatical terms are useful, but not strictly necessary for you to understand what Dickens is doing):

> 'you was' – non standard agreement between subject and verb;
> 'I knowed' – an irregular verb used as though regular;
> 'you waits' – non standard agreement between subject and verb;
> 'thank'ee' – a written representation of accent;
> 'I don't complain of none' – use of double negative;
> 'alonger' – dialect word for alongside.

The use of dialect by Dickens is a way of representing Magwitch as a man of lower class; and anyway he has a criminal record which reinforces this view. But while his speech has many dialect features, it is also metaphorical:

> 'You always waits at the gate' is both literally the gate of prison, but also the metaphorical gate of heaven – Pip is an angel.

> 'You've been comfortable alonger me, since I was under a dark cloud, than when the sun shone' is a very obvious metaphor. Magwitch uses an image of light/dark and has the perception to see through Pip's behaviour.

What Dickens is doing is showing Magwitch as someone who has little outer sophistication, but who within himself can understand people through a sort of poetic insight. The fact that his crimes are unnamed, helps here – had Dickens created Magwitch as a violent uncaring murderer, for example, this later characterisation would have been harder to accept.

Pip is of course narrating this scene, but the crucial area to consider is his narrative standpoint. In other words this is not a simultaneous narrative, one that is being reported as it happens. Instead it is being narrated at a time well after the action; Pip is now much older and wiser than he was, and the real significance of what happened has already dawned on him. Although the metaphor Pip uses to describe Magwitch's eyes involves the idea of a film covering them, it is the film removed from Pip's eyes which really matters. Even the final paragraph, which seems to suggest that Pip was 'mindful, then' reinforces this view; the Biblical quotation is too neat, too reflective to be spontaneous.

This is a deathbed scene, itself an intertextual idea in that it carries certain audience expectations; repentance and/or reconciliation are two common fictional uses of such scenes. This is not quite the case here in that the reconciliation has already taken place. It is, instead, a leave-taking, but one in which both participants learn something. Pip learns about love for others, regardless of social status, and Magwitch learns that not only is his daughter alive, but that she is in love with Pip. He dies happy in this knowledge. Note too how the governor and jailer are seen to detect this mood and move out of the scene.

How you respond to this depends on various contextual factors. Dickens' Victorian readers would almost certainly have approved, and Dickens, as a professional writer making a living from his works, knew how to give his audience what they wanted. Modern readers may be less comfortable with the neatness of it all – everything that needs to be said is said, nobody gets in the way or interrupts, love is seen as triumphant and God forgives a sinner. Modern readers' problems with this are a good example of the way readers' responses can change over time, and this can be further illustrated by looking at the way Peter Carey uses Dickens' novel to very different effect.

Task – Jack Maggs

Peter Carey is Australian. When interviewed about the novel he said:

> Dickens, in writing about this convict from Australia, Magwitch, was in a sense writing about my ancestor. *Great Expectations* is a great novel, but to an Australian it shows the way the English have colonised our ways of seeing ourselves. *Great Expectations* is a prison, and *Jack Maggs* is an attempt to break open the prison.

Carey is not re-writing Dickens' novel from a new perspective, but the fact that he is using it intertextually will be evident from a brief outline of part of his novel: Maggs returns to London to find his 'son' Henry Phipps, who thanks to Maggs' financial support has taken up a life of decadence and gay sex. Maggs meets a struggling novelist, Tobias Oates, who hypnotises Maggs in an attempt to steal his experiences to put in his next novel. Maggs in turn discovers the novelist's secrets and blackmails him in an attempt to find the ungrateful Phipps.

There are obvious similarities between the two texts. The names of Maggs and Phipps are close to the originals, and a figure very similar to Dickens – Tobias Oates – is also placed inside the story. The Victorian settings are often similar too. On the other hand, Carey makes a new story; Phipps and Maggs do not meet, and the presentation of sex and sexuality in the novel reflects late twentieth-century fiction rather than Victorian.

The following extract comes at a point where Maggs is still trying to meet Phipps. He sends him, via a character called Constable, gifts and letters which are written in invisible ink.

Read the extract carefully, at least twice, and then make notes, ideally in a group, on the following questions:

1   How does Carey present the character of Phipps in this extract?
2   How does the relationship in this extract differ from the one presented in *Great Expectations* above?
3   Look again at Carey's comment above about the novel. By seeing Phipps as a representation of England and Maggs, of Australia, can you interpret this extract as a comment on colonialism?

Text   *Jack Maggs*

'And the largest of the three, so I understand, is a certain document which Mr Maggs would have you read.'

Constable then held out all three parcels.

'A legal document?' asked Henry Phipps, unable to hide his growing excitement.

'No, I think not.'

'Not the title to a house, for instance?'

'I imagine it is a sort of letter.'

'A letter?' cried Henry Phipps, suddenly angry. 'Do you think I could correspond with such a one as he? And do you not consider the doubtful position you place yourself in? You are breaking the law to know his whereabouts without disclosing it. He is a dangerous man, Mr Racehorse, a man condemned to banishment, for ever. If you wish to reveal my presence to him, I swear I will make you wish that you were never born.'

'Sir, my information is that he sits up half the night writing in order to explain himself to you.'

'He said this?'

'Please, Sir, he thinks only of you. If ever he did you harm, I am very sure that he is sorry.'

For the third time, Constable attempted to deliver Jack Maggs's gifts.

'He says it is necessary to squeeze a little lemon juice upon the pages. And then to read them through the mirror image.' There was a pause. 'He is very fond of you.'

'But I am not fond of him. Tell him that I find the very notion of him vile.'

'Can I give him no comfort?'

'Yes: you may tell him that I am well aware of the obligation he has placed me under, and that he can therefore rely upon my silence for the moment.'

And with that the interview ended, and Henry Phipps strode from the room.

Commentary

The first things to note here are how the narrative techniques differ in each extract. Instead of a reflective first person narrative, this time the narrative is in the third person, and very sparely used. Nearly all of the extract consists of dialogue between Phipps and Constable, and although we hear about Maggs, he is not present. The narrative provides no commentary or interpretation, merely details of physical action.

Phipps is exposed through the dialogue. He is greedy, interested in legal documents which may lead to money, and self-centred, uninterested in letters and communication for its own sake. He looks down on 'such a one' as Maggs and is prepared to exploit the fact that he is a convict, even though he is prepared to keep quiet 'for the moment'. He finds the very notion of fondness 'vile'.

The sentimentality noted in the Dickens extract is distinctly absent here. Phipps is aloof, scheming, rude, aggressive and thoroughly unpleasant. Even by reading this extract, it is hard not to feel sympathy for Maggs, who spends 'half the night writing in order to explain himself to you'. Phipps seems utterly unworthy of such affection, yet is not surprised he receives it. He merely sees Maggs as beneath him, despite the wealth he has contributed.

In one sense, of course, this is a fictional exchange between invented characters. If you see Phipps and Maggs as representative characters, however, a further interpretation is possible, partly because we have no access to characters' thoughts, only to their words and actions.

If you read the following account of the relationship between Phipps and Maggs:

Phipps expects loyalty and generosity, but looks down on Maggs. Maggs provides Phipps with wealth. Maggs wants to impress Phipps, but is kept at a distance, provided he keeps coming up with the money. Phipps threatens Maggs with danger if he does not behave properly. Phipps will not meet Maggs directly, but will only deal with him through messengers.

and then re-read the acount, but this time replace the word 'Phipps' with the word 'England' and the word 'Maggs' with the word 'Australia' you can see how it is possible to read the extract as a comment on colonialism. The colonial power, England, exploits the colonised country, Australia, while at the same time looking down upon it as culturally inferior.

One way a colonial power imposes itself upon a colonised country is by imposing its language and its literature on the subjugated people. Carey uses aspects of the original novel, an English classic, but reshapes it in such a way that questions many of the unstated values and assumptions that informed the original novel.

The literary canon

For students of English Literature at GCSE and AS/A Level, studying literature involves reading a selection of books and writing about them. These books mainly come from set text lists. At GCSE, the National Curriculum specifies a list of authors from which teachers must choose. At AS/A Level lists are compiled by people who work for exam boards, but they do not have a completely free choice. Government rules lay down certain criteria which must apply. Some of these criteria are as follows:

- a Shakespeare play must be studied;
- different genres (i.e. poetry, prose and drama) must be studied, (Shakespeare does not count as drama);
- texts from certain historical times must be studied, i.e. pre-1770 and pre-1900;
- texts must have been written originally in English;
- texts must be of 'sufficient quality and substance to merit serious consideration'.

133

Task

The following questions are suitable for discussion in groups or for written answers.

1   To what extent do you agree that the categories above should be laid down by law?
2   Do any of the above categories seem to you to be problematic in any way?
3   Would you add any categories of your own?

Commentary

It can be argued that each of the above categories is at least questionable. Shakespeare is the only writer given unique status. Is he really that good? If he is, and you must study a play of his, rather than his poems, then why doesn't this play count as drama for the purposes of studying genre? After all, it must be a very good example of the genre if it is by the only author who is specifically named.

The word genre is itself problematic, as you will see later in this chapter. Here it is taken to mean a type of structure, and most students and teachers would probably agree that poems, novels and plays should all be studied. But the word genre can also be used to describe categories of content. Given that vast acres of bookshops are devoted to crime, science fiction, thrillers, romance etc., shouldn't they be included in the required list too? Shouldn't you have to study what is popularly read now, in the time in which you are living?

The requirement to read 'old' texts is seen as important because it gives students an understanding of literary heritage, often associated with a sense of national history, of 'our' past. But is this whole heritage, covering over 600 years of writing, really served by reading just a couple of randomly chosen books? And anyway, aren't dates arbitrary? Thomas Hardy put a date at the end of his poem about the end of the nineteenth century, *The Darkling Thrush*; this date was 'December 31 1900.' He thought he was writing on the last day of the nineteenth century, but this poem would not count as pre-1900 according to the current rules. Likewise, 1770 seems an oddly arbitrary date to choose as a time barrier.

If you are studying English Literature, it might seem reasonable to expect the texts to be written in English. But again, is it so clear-cut? Some of the most performed plays in this country are by

Chekhov and Ibsen – but they can no longer be studied at A Level. The recent poet laureate Ted Hughes wrote a hugely acclaimed volume of poems called *Tales from Ovid;* but as these are translations they presumably cannot count either.

The final category listed above – whether or not a text is of sufficient literary substance – is the hardest of all to take without question. What is meant by 'substance', and who decides? Are science books/travel books/religious books/children's books allowed to be literature? Is substance judged by popularity, by book sales, by readership figures or by self-appointed judges?

The following appeared recently in a magazine for A level students. The author, writing about spy novels, said:

> Clancy never seriously questions the American way of life, Fleming and Forsyth are scarcely George Eliot, and le Carré can write very badly on occasions – in other words Cold War novels commonly fail to meet the standards of great literature.
>
> C. Butler, *The English Review*, Vol. 10 (1), Sept. 1999

Three reasons are given for rejecting spy novels as 'great literature': first, because there is an absence of certain social comment; second, because they are not like a certain Victorian novelist (or, presumably, her books); and third, because they are badly written. All of these reasons are subjective, showing the critic's preferences rather than any scientific proof. Is it possible in a single sentence to define good and bad writing? Do good writers have to make social comment? Is George Eliot a suitable point of comparison for writers of twentieth-century genre fiction?

So far, this commentary has invited you to question the rules governing the selection of texts. It can also be argued that other possible criteria are noticeably absent. There is no requirement to study books by women, nor is there any requirement to study authors who represent the ethnic diversity of writers in English. Should there be?

Defining 'Literature'

The word 'literature' has Latin origins. 'Littera' meant letter, and 'litteratura' meant knowledge of reading and writing. Gradually, during the seventeenth and eighteenth centuries, the word was applied to writing which was consciously stylish, often putting effect before meaning. At this time, the word was still applied to any writing on any topic. This usage remains when we refer to the literature that accompanies a specialist topic, i.e. 'I have read all the literature and have decided to go to Spain on holiday'.

By the mid-nineteenth century, the word 'literature' was being given a capital L and used to refer to writing in the forms of poetry, drama and novels, ranked in status in that order. Other writing, like biography, memoirs, diaries etc. were being pushed into the background, with only odd examples counting as Literature. Who decided what was and what was not Literature was in the hands of a few influential critics. Once Literature became a subject to be studied at school and university, whether a work was Literature or not depended on whether it was one of those chosen for study. Works that were allowed into Literature became known as the 'canon'.

There is, however, something very circular about the notion of literary quality and greatness. We know what literature is because we can name some great writers. We then judge other writers against these names to see if they match up. Literature is defined in *The New Oxford Dictionary* of 1998 as 'written works considered to be of superior or lasting merit'. But considered by whom? And how can you look into the future to know if a book will last? And does the fact that a book lasts, necessarily mean it is great?

Robert Eaglestone in his book *Doing English* points out that there is also something self-perpetuating about the canon. Teachers of English often teach the texts they were taught, while students (and their parents) will expect to study texts they have heard of, especially if they are having to pay tuition fees.

It is also worth remembering that attitudes and values lie behind the choice of texts which are allowed into the canon or on set book lists. These are sometimes open and explicit, such as the inclusion of women writers or black writers, but they are often more obscure, revolving around abstract concepts such as 'substance', 'significance', 'quality'. Whether explicit or not, conferring status on a text by putting it on a Literature course means that it has been identified by some group or other as confirming the values they hold.

Task

Which of the following texts or type of text would you consider suitable for an A Level Literature course, and which would you reject, bearing in mind that at A Level, far fewer texts are read than at degree level? Ideally this will be done in group discussion, but make sure that you give reasons for your choice. This task assumes that you have some knowledge of the texts. If you do not, you could try to find out about them through library or internet resources. Note that there is no commentary with this task.

The Taming of the Shrew – Shakespeare
Any book in the *Noddy* series – Enid Blyton
A Terry Pratchett novel
A *Harry Potter* story – J.K. Rowling
A Brief History of Time – Stephen Hawking
The Royle Family scripts – from the television series
A biography of Alan Shearer
V – a poem by Tony Harrison
A collection of limericks
The Political Diaries of Alan Clark
Titus Andronicus – Shakespeare

Literary language

Reference is made above to a circular argument: you can only say whether or not a work is of literary merit by comparing it to other works of literary merit which can be compared to others and so on. In other words, there is no definition of merit, only examples.

In order to tackle the problem faced by the circularity of the argument, some critics have argued that Literature is Literature because of its 'special' use of language, but with language too it can be argued that what are often claimed as distinctive features of literary language are in fact present in all sorts of everyday written and spoken texts which would not normally be termed Literature.

The critic Geoffrey Leech, writing in *A Linguistic Guide to English Poetry*, finds three broad features of what he calls poetic language. These are:

1   *repetition and parallelism*: patterns of repeated words, repeated sounds (alliteration, assonance, rhyme etc.), repeated grammar structures, semantic fields (i.e. words which cluster around the same area of meaning);
2   *deviation*: use of deliberately archaic words, invented 'new' words and languages, breaking of grammatical rules, unusual graphology (i.e. lay-out and appearance of a text);
3   *creativity*: metaphor and comparison, multiple meaning, ambiguity.

Examples from what are generally accepted as literary texts are:

Repetition and parallelism

> Tyger, tyger, burning bright,
> In the forest of the night:
>> William Blake

Deviation

> Do not go gentle into that good night,
>> Dylan Thomas

Creativity

> Our two souls therefore, which are one,
>> Though I must go, endure not yet
> A breach, but an expansion,
>> Like gold to airy thinness beat.
>>> John Donne

Task

For each of the above lines of poetry, show how they can be said to fit into the given category.

Commentary

The extract from Blake's poem *The Tyger* shows a number of features of repetition. The word 'tyger' is repeated and there is alliteration in 'burning bright'. The rhythm of both lines is also identical. Parallelism can be seen in the use of the rhyme 'bright/night'.

The line from Dylan Thomas shows grammatical deviation in the word 'gentle'. According to the strict rules of grammar, an adverb – 'gently' – should follow a verb. The deviation works, provided we understand that Thomas knows what he is doing and is deliberately breaking rules. If we think he has simply made a mistake, then we are unlikely to consider his poem to be literature.

The third text, which is about lovers parting, is ambiguous in that, having stated that they are two souls, it promptly says they are one. The simile is 'creative' in that it is unusual, referring to the beating of gold which, through being spread across a distance, does not break but actually improves in appearance.

These, then, are examples that fit Leech's categories. It is equally possible to find examples of the same linguistic features in what would be considered distinctly non-literary texts.

Repetition and parallelism

> Mile-High Mandy got randy on brandy
> > *Sun* headline, October 1999:
> > a woman was said to have had sex on a plane.

Deviation

> Clobba Slobba
> > *Sun* headline, March 1999:
> > urging Nato to bomb Serbia.

Creativity

> Hull 1   Crewe 1
> > Advertising slogan for Littlewoods Pools,
> > showing a 'winner' on board a luxury yacht.

It would seem, then, that distinctive features of language are not, in themselves, sufficient to turn a text into a part of the literary canon.

Task

1   Return to the *Nurofen* advert on page 35. To what extent can features of poetic language, as described above, be seen in this text?
2   Again using the categories above, find further examples of your own, drawing upon what are commonly seen as literary and non-literary texts.

There is no commentary with this task.

Genre and subgenre

It was noted above that one use of the word genre refers to very broad definitions of types of text; poetry, prose and drama. Essentially this use of the term defines the form of writing that has been used. Actually defining these forms is problematic, not least because they often overlap. Shakespeare writes plays which include poetry and prose; some novelists' prose is often described as poetic, and so on.

It is also obvious that these three categories have many subcategories within them. Radio drama is very different from television drama, which is different again from film drama, which is different from stage drama. The latter subcategory, stage drama, tends to have higher status than the others, presumably because it is the older form.

You will notice that the way the genres of drama were separated in the previous paragraph was through difference. It would seem therefore that the two key factors which determine the way we categorise texts is through **difference** and **similarity**. If one text differs from another, then they do not belong in the same category. If, on the other hand, they are similar, then they can be put in the same category. In reality, of course, it is never this easy. If two texts are the same in every way, then they will be identical. As soon as texts differ in one way or another, then they can be categorised apart.

It has already been noted that official criteria for what must be studied at A Level includes the genres of prose, poetry and drama. This alone is not enough; not just any old poetry, prose or drama can be studied – further categories are needed. These categories are concerned with 'quality', 'substance' and 'merit', and it is here that the real problem arises. While some categories are reasonably uncontentious, others are not so. If a small number of people are able to decide what is and what is not 'quality', 'substance' and 'merit', they have a huge amount of power to shape our culture through what is read in school and college.

Task

A useful way of considering aspects of canon and genre is to take an example from television. Make a list of all the quiz shows that are on television, and make lists of as many subgenres as you can. Try to place the same programmes into different categories, so that you show programmes interconnecting in different ways.

Commentary

It is likely that within the major genre of quiz show, you have found very different programmes. *University Challenge* (a very old format) differs in many ways from *Who Wants to be a Millionnaire* (very popular at the time of writing, but perhaps soon to wane). Both programmes have a quizmaster who asks questions, a very important structural similarity, but in other ways they have many differences.

Some of the categories you may have formed are:

long-established quiz shows or new quiz shows
quiz shows for individuals
quiz shows for teams
quiz shows for big cash prizes
quiz shows with small prizes
quiz shows with multiple choice questions
quiz shows with visual questions
quiz shows based on words/vocabulary
general knowledge quiz shows
specialist knowledge quiz shows
quiz shows with studio audiences
quiz shows without studio audiences
quiz shows for a specific age group
quiz shows for a broadly based audience
quiz shows made by the same production team

What emerges in general terms from this list is that subgenres can be formed through:

◎   similarity of **form** (i.e. with a studio audience);
◎   similarity of **content** (i.e. general knowledge quiz shows);
◎   similarity of **purpose** (i.e. to inform as well as entertain)
◎   similarity of **audience** (i.e. designed for a specific age group);
◎   similarity of **time** (i.e. belonging to the same period);
◎   similarity of **production** (i.e. made by the same people).

Although you may have formed a subgenre called 'popularity', based upon the viewing figures for each programme, it is highly unlikely that you have formed sub-genres based upon quality, substance or merit, which, ironically, appear too vague and insubstantial to be used in this way.

To translate the ideas about quiz shows to literary texts, what has emerged so far is that:

◎   texts can be categorised by form, content, purpose, audience, time of production, authorship;
◎   categorisation involves similarity and difference
◎   these categories or subgenres are not fixed;
◎   texts can move around various categories;
◎   categories based upon personal values are not valid for everyone.

141

A literary subgenre – bird poems

The way we categorise texts reflects issues of the culture in which we live. Categorisation is a group activity allowing us to share a view of a text with someone else. Part of what we do when we read any text is to place it mentally alongside other texts we have read before.

In order to give an example of a literary subgenre, some poems about birds will now be explored. Before doing this, we need to explore some of the ways we collectively view birds in our culture. For a more detailed analysis of birds in popular culture, see the chapter 'Signs and Sounds' in *Working with Texts* (Routledge, Carter, Goddard et al.).

Task

1   For each of the following birds, say what connotations (i.e. associations) come to mind, and then, if possible, why you think these connotations exist.
     a cuckoo
     a magpie
     a swallow
     a sparrow
     an eagle

2   Why do you think so many poets have written about birds?

Commentary

The cuckoo seems to have two distinct and opposite connotations in our culture. On the one hand it is positive, heralding the arrival of spring. Hearing the first cuckoo is a time of joy. On the other hand, it is an invader, something that sponges off others, hence our use of the word 'cuckoo' to suggest someone who is invading our territory.

The magpie is known for its thieving, its ugly song and its aggression. For most people this bird has negative connotations, but for fans of Newcastle United, nicknamed 'The Magpies', who wear black and white stripes as a badge of honour, this bird will also have much more positive connotations.

The swallow for most people is about speed and grace. It would be hard to conceive of a poem about a swallow which treated the bird negatively. A sparrow, on the other hand, is cheeky, full of character, essentially urban. An eagle, although most of us have never seen one, is regal, powerful, above us all in every way.

In making these broad assertions about what are, after all, merely birds, we are using shared cultural ideas. We are seeing these birds not literally but metaphorically, using them as reference points for our own experience. By linking birds to human qualities we are **anthropomorphising** them; when you think about it, it is not possible to believe that sparrows are in reality cheeky, because cheekiness is itself a human quality.

There are a number of possible reasons why birds are so frequently used in poetry. These include:

◎   they are common points of reference for readers, who can be assumed to recognise them;
◎   they fly (which we cannot) above us, and height is a common metaphor for superiority, religious values etc.;
◎   they tend to be small and fragile, usually harmless to humans;
◎   they produce musical song – never mind that this is usually an aggressive territorial act.

Task

The two following poems are both clearly about birds. Read them carefully and then prepare answers to the following questions:

1   The poem taken from *Auguries of Innocence*, by William Blake, refers to a number of birds. (An augury is a sign, a symbol.) What use does Blake make of the birds here?
2   How do you interpret the use of the bird in *Sparrow*, by Norman MacCaig?
3   To what extent can these two poems be placed in the same subgenre, and to what extent are they different from each other?

from *Auguries of Innocence*

A Robin Redbreast in a cage
Puts all Heaven in a rage.

A Dove house filled with Doves and Pigeons
Shudders hell through all its regions.

A Skylark wounded in the wing
A cherubin does cease to sing.

The Game Cock clipped and armed to fight
Does the rising sun affright.

The Bat that flits at close of eve
has left the brain that won't believe.

The Owl that calls upon the night
Speaks the unbeliever's fright.

William Blake

Sparrow

He's no artist.
His taste in clothes is more
dowdy than gaudy.
And his nest – that blackbird, writing
pretty scrolls on the air with the gold nib of his beak,
would call it a slum.

To stalk solitary on lawns,
to sing solitary in midnight trees,
to glide solitary over gray Atlantics –
not for him: he'd rather
a punch-up in a gutter.

He carries what learning he has
lightly – it is in fact, based only
on the usefulness whose result
is survival. A proletarian bird.
No scholar.

But when winter soft-shoes in
and these other birds –
ballet dancers, musicians, architects –
die in the snow
and freeze to branches,
watch him happily flying
on the O-levels and A-levels
of the air.

Norman MacCaig

Commentary

The first poem, as usual with Blake, is open to a range of interpretations. Each verse takes a well-known British bird, and in its strong rhymes and rhythm seems to make a different point about innocence, itself an elusive concept. Here are some interpretations for each verse, but you may well have found others.

The caged robin is an affront to Heaven, because birds should fly free. This verse could refer to the way humanity abuses the world by trying to control nature, but if we see flight as having a religious dimension, as being spiritual, then this could be an attack on religious intolerance, where organised religion puts belief in a straight-jacket.

The second verse refers to hell, and we usually associate doves (but not pigeons?) with peace. So a 'house filled' with doves shows an innocent and popular desire for peace. Hell is a place of war, inhabited by those, such as politicians, who thrive on conflict. Again, this idea of conflict could be applied as much to religion as to politics.

The skylark is noted for its sudden flight and glorious song. If it is wounded, perhaps on a literal level by men shooting at it, then here is another example of heaven being affronted – this time because a cherubin or angel stops singing.

The Game Cock too is altered by the actions of man, and becomes a symbol of war and conflict. Frightening the rising sun suggests that the most routine of natural things can be symbolically perverted by humans.

Both the Owl and the Bat (note how all the birds are given capital letters) are night creatures, and both are linked in this poem by the idea of non-belief. The poem began with the possible idea of religious intolerance, a failure to see beyond a cage. Here unbelievers are seen in a similar way, as they too are in a sense locked into a narrow view. Blake does not say unbelief in what, just unbelief itself, and the poem ends on the word 'fright', a deliberately unsettling closure.

MacCaig's sparrow moves from a series of negative comparisons at the beginning of the poem to something much more positive at the end. The sparrow is given its singular identity through comparison (a) to other birds and (b) to humans. The references to other birds contain potential references to other poems about birds: Keats's *Ode to a Nightingale* could be the reference in 'to sing solitary in midnight trees', while the bird gliding 'solitary over gray Atlantics' could be the albatross in Coleridge's *Rime of the Ancient Mariner*. The sparrow lacks the glamorous colours of other birds, its nest is messy, it has none of

145

the solitary splendour of more romanticised birds; it is more communal, favouring a 'punch-up' in a gutter.

At this point the human comparisons are made, largely through the idea of learning and scholarship. This bird is 'no scholar', yet it is a survivor, and while all others are failing, it flies along the various 'levels/of the air'.

Although there is plenty of anthropomorphism here – the bird is quite clearly seen in very human terms – the purpose of this anthropomorphism is more ambiguous. Usually birds are used by poets to explore something about the human condition, in the way Blake does, but here it could be argued that human activity is used to locate the specific features of a bird. In other words it really is about a sparrow. It would be perfectly possible, though, to produce a reading of the poem which suggested that the sparrow is used in a similarly symbolic way to Blake's birds, and that the sparrow is representing people who are not highly educated, but who are better adapted to life than those who are educated in traditional ways.

It was made clear earlier in this chapter that genres and subgenres work through a sense of difference and similarity. On a simple level these two poems can be put into a category called 'bird poems'. Whether or not these two poems can be placed together in other ways depends upon your readings of them. Genres, like meanings, are not fixed. Our desire to 'place' texts by putting them alongside others is, in a sense, offset by the way we, both as individuals and collectively, read the texts in different ways. This tension between similarity and difference is one of the most important factors in our reading.

Task

1   As an extension of the work done here on two bird poems, collect further examples yourself and see how far you can categorise poems together or apart. There are literally hundreds of poems to choose from, so finding them should not be a problem.
2   Another way of identifying issues of genre and text is to deliberately 'play' with texts by presenting them through the conventions of other genres. To do this effectively, of course, you need to have a clear focus on the original text, and a sure sense of the genre conventions you are 'moving' it to.

Using some of the texts in this book, re-present them in a different genre or genres. Some possibilities are :

- Mr Bleaney's post-card to his landlady from Frinton;
- *Sense and Sensibility* as a script for *The Money Programme*;
- *Sparrow* as an entry in a child's book of birds;
- Robinson Crusoe and Friday both interviewed for the magazine series *How We Met*.

Conclusion

This chapter has focused on three connected ideas: intertextuality; what constitutes the so-called literary canon; and how readers place texts through ideas of genre. Both canon and genre have been seen to be more tricky than is sometimes suggested. The canon as a concept is problematic because it is based upon dubious criteria of choice, and notions of genre are problematic because texts can move around and within genres in various ways. The common idea then, linking the three parts of this chapter, is that although Literature courses seem to have some clearly fixed points – quality books from a range of genres – these are not really fixed points at all. Instead they are more subjective than is often claimed, and based upon assumptions and values that need at least to be questioned.

In terms of the context outline that informs this book as a whole, this chapter has focused in particular on **the texts's context** and **the reader's context**. Whether or not a text is seen to be in the canon, to be of 'sufficient quality and substance to merit serious consideration', clearly affects the way it is perceived by its readers. Our ability to read objectively a text that we already have been told is 'great' is going to be in some ways limited. The placing of a text in a category of greatness is an act governed by cultural assumptions and values. Predetermining that texts are 'great' is a conservative action; it supports the cultural values that currently exist rather than questions them.

The part of the chapter which has dealt with notions of genre has again drawn upon **the texts's context** and **the reader's context**. In addition it has referred to the idea of generic conventions of form and language, so referring to **the language context**, with obvious connections to ideas of intertextuality. Additionally, notions of genre have been explored through two poems which have ambig-uous connections. This notion of ambiguity, of where a text belongs in relation to other texts, is part of **the readings context**.

Chapter *nine*

Critical viewpoints

This final chapter will draw together the various strands of the book by looking at one text, *The Going* by Thomas Hardy, from a number of different viewpoints. This process will:

1   Enable you to revise many of the issues that have been dealt with earlier, especially in preparation for exams. In particular this should help you with the synoptic elements of A Level.
2   Show you how your readings of a text can be shaped by various factors at work both inside and outside the text.

The first readings

The first part of this process involves acquainting yourself with the text by reading it a number of times and by forming some initial responses. This first meeting with the text is crucial, because it will provide you with ideas that will have to be tested against further evidence as it accumulates.

Task

1   Read the poem at least twice, jotting down any initial thoughts and ideas. Your very first reading will inevitably focus on what the text is 'about'. Although this idea of content will inevitably

149

shift and move, without an initial overview based on subject-matter, you are always going to struggle.

2   Now after a second reading look at some broad features of form and language, such as the way the text begins and ends, some features that distinguish it as a poem, any verbal patterns that you can easily find.

Text   *The Going*

Why did you give no hint that night
That quickly after the morrow's dawn,
And calmly, as if indifferent quite,
You would close your term here, up and be gone
        Where I could not follow
        With wing of swallow
To gain one glimpse of you ever anon!

        Never to bid good-bye,
        Or lip me the softest call,
Or utter a wish for a word, while I
Saw morning harden upon the wall,
        Unmoved, unknowing
        That your great going
Had place that moment, and altered all.

Why do you make me leave the house
And think for a breath it is you I see
At the end of the alley of bending boughs
Where so often at dusk you used to be;
        Till in darkening dankness
        The yawning blankness
Of the perspective sickens me!

        You were she who abode
        By those red-veined rocks far West
You were the swan-necked one who rode
Along the beetling Beeny Crest,
        And, reining nigh me,
        Would muse and eye me,
While life unrolled us its very best.

150

Why, then, latterly did we not speak,
Did we not think of those days long dead,
And ere your vanishing strive to seek
That time's renewal? We might have said,
    'In this bright spring weather
    We'll visit together
Those places that once we visited.'

    Well, well! All's past amend,
    Unchangeable. It must go.
I seem but a dead man held on end
To sink down soon ... O you could not know
    That such swift fleeing
    No soul foreseeing -
Not even I – would undo me so!

(December 1912)

Commentary

Some of the subject matter which you will probably have noticed is as follows:

◎   the poem is addressed to a 'you' who has gone, hence the title;
◎   the 'you' left quickly without saying good-bye;
◎   the departure has devastated the persona narrating the poem;
◎   the persona still searches for the 'you', even though this is fruit-less;
◎   the departed one is a woman, who is remembered in a sort of perfect past;
◎   recent times between the two were less successful;
◎   the persona is resigned to her going, but broken by it too;
◎   in some way, not yet fully defined, this can be categorised as a love poem.

Some of the presentational features you may have noticed include:

◎   this is a poem with certain structures such as verses and rhymes;
◎   there are many different words for the idea of 'going';
◎   it sounds at times as though the persona is accusing the woman;
◎   there are several different time-scales in the poem;
◎   the poem is given a specific date.

What we have here is a love poem, where the narrative persona has been deserted and feels a deep sense of loss. In what sense the woman has 'gone' is not really clear.

First readings inevitably lead us to search for a core of meaning and of form, and placing a text in a category gives us a comfort zone by allowing us to say that the text is like others that we have known and processed. In many texts that we encounter every day, that is enough, but moving beyond that comfort zone, finding more than the bare minimum, is necessary if the text's full potential is to be explored.

This metaphor of exploration, often used in the trigger part of exam questions in the instruction to 'explore', is worth considering briefly. Explorers go into uncharted lands, where nobody has been before, not knowing what they will find, but knowing that they are going to be stretched to the limits. They will be well-trained and well-equipped, but alert to the unexpected. Exploring a text involves metaphorically the same ideas: you have practised the skills, you are well-informed of the techniques, your previous experience means that you have broad ideas of what to expect, yet you also know you will face something new and unknown.

The next readings

Having noted some tentative findings about the poem on first readings, these now need to be examined in rather more detail. The metaphor of examination, just used here, is another favourite trigger in questions – questions which are themselves part of an examination. The root meaning of the word 'examine' goes back to its Latin origins, suggesting weighing or balancing, and thus by extension looking at closely.

Task

1   Examine the range of expressions used by Hardy for the idea of the loved one going/departing, and the effect of this departure on the person left behind.
2   Examine aspects of time as presented in the poem.

Commentary

One of the major findings of the first reading was that from the title onwards, there was a range of expressions for the idea of the loved one going or departing. These are:

> 'going'
> 'close your term here, up'
> 'be gone'
> 'never to bid good-bye'
> 'great going'
> 'your vanishing'
> 'swift fleeing'

Various semantic fields are opened up here: there are ideas of speed of departure; unexpectedness of departure; running away; 'greatness'; and the rather unusual idea of a 'term', a fixed period being closed.

Another area to notice at this point is the language used to describe the effect of the departure on the person left behind.

◎ Now she has gone the 'yawning blankness/Of the perspective sickens me!', the hard 'k' sounds giving added weight to the expression of feeling;
◎ a resignation that 'All's past amend,/Unchangeable.';
◎ 'I seem but a dead man';
◎ 'would undo me so!'.

The final words of the poem express a sense of devastation at what has happened.

The third area to notice involves aspects of time, some of which are indicated by verb tenses and others through more direct reference to past events.

◎ the 'Going' of the title, although used as a noun, carries some suggestion of continuous time, of still going on now;
◎ 'that night'/'morrow's dawn'/'that moment' are specific time references in one sense, but not identifiable by the reader;
◎ 'ever anon', meaning ever again, suggests the future;
◎ 'make me leave'/'sickens me' is in the fictional present of the poem, with a strong suggestion of repeated action;
◎ 'You were she who abode' is a distant past to be compared with …

153

◎   ... 'latterly' which is the past, but a more recent past;
◎   'we might have said' is a conditional past tense – it was possible but did not happen;
◎   'We'll visit together/Those places that once we visited' is what might have been said but was not, containing a possible future linked to a distant past;
◎   the poem ends in the fictional present with 'I seem but a dead man';
◎   the poem is then given a specific date.

This appears quite complex when put together in a list, but essentially there are four time scales at work: the distant past; the recent past; the present; and the future. Each of these four time scales is accompanied by an emotional identification:

◎   the distant past involved life at its 'very best';
◎   the recent past involved 'not speak(ing)';
◎   the present involves brief illusion before 'yawning blankness';
◎   the future is 'unchangeable'.

To summarise, we have a poem of lost love, of lost opportunity, of despair and pain. This, like many love poems, is about hurt and pain, with hints at something better in the distant past. We have reached this reading through close attention to features that are *in* the poem, such as its language and its structure through reference to time. For followers of the school of **practical criticism** this would be enough; the text is taken in isolation and, by applying methodical scrutiny, an understanding has been reached. This approach to literature was (and maybe still is in one or two places) the mainstay of study, culminating in what was often known as the 'unseen' exam paper.

This book has argued, though, that we not only need to look at what is *in* the text, but what goes *with* it – in other words aspects of *context*. These will now follow the preliminary readings.

The author's context/the text's context

These two aspects of context are inevitably close together and often interlock. We now need to see how our current readings of the poem are affected by some added information.

Context 1

This poem is the first of a sequence called *Poems 1912–13*. Hardy gave the whole sequence a Latin epigraph *Veteris vestigia flammae*, which means 'Traces of an ancient flame'. They were written in the months after the death of his wife Emma, who died on 27 November 1912. This poem, then, was written very soon after Emma died. Hardy himself was 72 at the time.

Task

How does this information affect possible readings of the poem so far?

Commentary

Having this information allows us to realise that the idea of going/departure in fact refers to death. We may have had an inkling of this from the phrase 'close your term here, up', but the fact that the word 'death' or other close variants does not appear anywhere in the poem takes on a special significance. All the words for 'going' become **euphemisms** for something much stronger. We are entitled to wonder why Hardy avoids the blunt reality of death – there seems to be some sort of avoidance taking place.

The fact that Hardy was 72 at the time gives some explanation for the different time scales, especially the two pasts – the distant past and the recent past.

Context 2

At the time of her death, Emma and her husband were estranged. Although living in the same house, they rarely spoke. Hardy had for some time been in a relationship with a much younger woman called Florence Dugdale, having previously been linked with other women.

As Hardy's fame had grown through the success of his novels, so Emma's behaviour had grown more eccentric. There are various theories as to why their marriage broke down: Hardy was an agnostic, his wife very pious; she looked down upon his rural origins; they were sexually incompatible; she envied his fame. Whatever the reasons, and in Victorian times there was no public dissection of marital breakdown, as Hardy's fame grew, and he became a figure in literary society, Emma, who herself had literary pretensions, grew more and more bitter. For thirty years they lived in disharmony.

Emma, who was the same age as Hardy, had for some years been suffering from an unpleasant illness. When she died, it was after a lot of suffering and was in no sense unexpected.

After her death, Hardy found diary entries called 'What I think of my husband' in which Emma wrote damningly of her husband. Hardy put these down to hallucinations and destroyed them.

This version of Hardy's relationship with his wife is the standard one in most biographies, which tend to see the relationship from his perspective rather than from Emma's. Whatever the 'truth' of their relationship, there can be little doubt that after early years of court-ship – they knew each other four years before marrying – there was great antipathy between the two in later years.

We have already noted that it is perfectly possible to respond to *The Going* without any biographical background. And biographical knowledge of the author can be an actual hindrance to the study of texts if it replaces analysis of the texts themselves. Yet once we know even the bare outlines of Hardy and Emma, as detailed above, it becomes impossible to read the poem in the same way that we did before knowing this information.

Task

Re-read the poem in the light of what you now know and make notes on how possible readings of the poem have further changed.

Commentary

The new contextual knowledge explains some things, and makes others more puzzling. The different time scales now fall into place, corresponding with phases in their relationship. References to their courtship in verse four, their more recent lack of communication, her failure to 'bid good-bye', all now make sense within the contextual knowledge we have acquired. And, of course, we know that talk of her 'going' refers to her death.

On the other hand, puzzles remain: one involves the apparent surprise Hardy feels at the 'going'. Surely if she had been ill for many years, even if he largely ignored her, he would know death was possible at any time? Another puzzle involves the depth of his feeling, the strength of lines such as 'The yawning blankness/Of the perspec-tive sickens me'. Why is he so devastated by the death of a woman he has not loved in years?

Context 3

The location for this poem is Hardy's home and garden in Dorset, but in the early months of 1913 Hardy set out on a pilgrimage to Cornwall, revisiting many of the places where he and Emma had gone during their courtship. Many of the poems in the sequence *Poems 1912–13* relate to specific places in Cornwall.

For a number of years Hardy had been in a relationship with Florence Dugdale. Although she was ostensibly a secretarial assistant, rumours abounded that they were lovers. Soon after Emma's death, Florence Dugdale moved into Hardy's house, and in 1914 they married. Hardy was 73, Florence 35. Florence Dugdale, in her role as Hardy's assistant, would have helped process the manuscripts of the poems in honour of his dead wife.

After Hardy's death, Florence published *The Life of Thomas Hardy*, claiming it to be her own work, but it was almost certainly dictated by Hardy himself.

Task

Re-read the poem in the light of what you now know and make notes on whether still further changes/additions can be made to the possible readings of the poem.

Commentary

What we have here is more biographical evidence of the apparent contradictions we have found in the poem. The introduction of ideas about infidelity before Emma's death, and re-marriage after it, make the idea of simple grief less acceptable. This could lead to a reading of the poem which makes guilt its dominant emotion. Although Hardy does not and maybe cannot mention such a feeling in the poem, the reader, equipped with information about his life, would certainly be justified in seeing this as a poem which is about Hardy's guilt at the way he had treated his wife.

The reader's context

It is unlikely that many modern readers will be surprised by a story of marital breakdown. What is more surprising is that it is the long-rejected partner whose death causes such an outpouring of grief. How

157

you respond to this poem, knowing something of its contextual background, depends upon your own attitudes and values.

Task

Write down your 'reading' of the poem in full, now that you have received the three sets of biographical material.

Commentary

Some responses by other students include:

◎ seeing the poem as a very poignant expression of a sensitive individual's turmoil when faced with extreme emotional circumstances;

◎ seeing the poem as a product of its time and contrasting the 'hints' of marital and even sexual tension with how such issues would be treated today;

◎ seeing the poem as an exercise in guilt, with Hardy attempting to come to terms with his past behaviour;

◎ seeing the poem as an exercise in guilt, but taking this further and suggesting that the guilt turns into a sort of mythologising, a re-inventing of the relationship;

◎ seeing the poem as essentially cynical, a public exercise in re-writing history, preparing the ground for the next relationship.

These interpretations, based in part upon what the students themselves are bringing to the poem, lead inevitably to an exploration of the readings context.

The readings context

Throughout this book you have been urged to see meaning as something that is neither fixed nor limited. The student responses noted above are not mutually exclusive. Each of them comes in part from the approach favoured by individual readers, and these readers have been affected by critical methods that they have picked up during their study of literature.

Although there are generic names for various critical approaches to texts, it is certainly not necessary to know these names in order to read texts in various ways. Indeed at A Level, trying to use theories that are only half-understood can get in the way of actually looking at the text, and even at undergraduate level intelligent reading is more important than academic labels. So, although some references will be made to different critical approaches, the main point to stress here is that a number of meanings can be found in *The Going*, and that it is perfectly possible to engage with them all at the same time, even if, as an individual reader, you find some more convincing than others.

Rob Pope in *The English Studies Book* distinguishes between what he calls *theory* and *practice*. *Theory* he defines as a 'systematic *reflection* upon methods and models', in other words an abstract process, whereas *practice* he defines as the 'application of general methods and models', which is a more active process. Ideally, as students of literature at this level, you will know enough about different ways of reading texts to become what Pope calls a 'reflective practitioner', without feeling the need to attach anything other than broad labels to the approach you have taken.

One approach to reading text, which was called **practical criticism,** has already been noted, and formed the early part of this chapter. The poem *The Going* was explored in detail through its language and structure, and important evidence was found. But evidence for what? Without the contextual material, the poem was only understood at one level – nothing was challenged. Indeed although exam papers in practical criticism often asked the students for a personal opinion, what on earth could they base this opinion on, without any contextual material to work with? There was also an assumption with this approach that the text had 'merit', otherwise why would it have been selected in the first place?

An **historical** approach to this poem would attempt to place the subject matter – marital break-down, guilt – within a broader historical framework of marriage as an institution in late Victorian times. Although this historical perspective can be useful, it is very easy for students to take it too far, presenting potted history in place of textual analysis. If an historical context helps us to find a meaning now, it can be useful. Using historical information in an attempt to find a definitive meaning of a text in its own time is necessarily doomed to failure.

In this poem, then, we see a man whose sense of loss and guilt comes from living within a moral code which was strict and unforgiving. Marriage was for life, whatever unhappiness it led to. The fact that Hardy grieves for a wife he did not love is part of the guilt-process which made this view of marriage so hard to break down.

Linked closely to this view of the text through an historical perspective is a **marxist** reading of the poem. A Marxist reading of the poem would look at the tyranny of the institution of marriage, and place this tyranny within a broader political perspective. Not only is Hardy a victim of a social institution, but this institution serves to maintain the power structure of the ruling class. Provincial, small-town Hardy is in no place to challenge a system which brings with it nothing but misery. This poem can be seen not as an expression of personal grief but as a powerless outcry against social injustice, made all the more poignant because Hardy does not see that for himself. As far as Hardy is concerned, the problem is his alone, when in reality the problem belongs to all who are repressed.

This view that the individual has no unique quality, that we are part of a socially constructed world, is in opposition to a **humanist** view, which takes the uniqueness of the individual as its starting point. The first student response noted above – that the poem is a very poignant expression of a sensitive individual's turmoil when faced with extreme emotional circumstances – comes in this category. This approach would use the biographical information to produce a reading of the poem which explored the 'nature' of Hardy's grief. As with the historical approach, this can be dangerous, even if you accept that it is possible to define the 'nature' of someone else's experience. There are two reasons for this approach being problematic: it is very easy for students to reproduce extensive biographical material with little reference to the text; and/or it is very tempting to match an incident in the author's life with an incident in a text as though they are *necessarily* connected.

With *The Going*, that temptation is especially strong because Hardy makes the poem seem so personal: his immediate address to 'you' in the first line; his dating of the poem at the end, are just two examples. And the many biographies of Hardy mean the information is readily accessible. In following this approach, we must remember that Hardy is not presenting us with his 'real' experience. He is presenting us with a *version* of his experience which he has shaped in a highly specific way. This poem, with its many internal patterns and structures, is made to resemble experience. We should pay as much attention to how he does this, as to what he says.

The third student response noted above – seeing the poem as an exercise in guilt, with Hardy attempting to come to terms with his past behaviour – is broadly speaking based upon a **psychological** approach to the text. Psychology can be defined as the study of the human mind and the way it affects behaviour in a given context. It is concerned with mass behaviour rather than individual behaviour; the latter, especially when associated with illness, is known as psychoanalysis.

For many years students of literature were asked to do a 'character study' or to answer questions on characters' motives, as though characters in (usually) novels were somehow real. This amateur psychoanalysis has largely been discredited, and you should avoid the temptation to approach what is clearly an autobiographical poem by claiming to know Hardy's state of mind. This does not mean that you cannot look at *The Going* from a more broadly-based psychological perspective.

Certainly one strong feature of this poem is its sense of absence, of avoidance of certain things. It does not mention the word death, and it alludes to problems in the relationship rather than highlighting them. 'Why then latterly did we not speak ... of those days long dead' suggests a relationship in crisis, but the way the poem is organised, with each verse treating a different aspect of the 'story' means that such references are hints at problems rather than full admissions of them.

If certain things are absent, then it is quite likely that there may be additions, a re-creation of events to suit a particular purpose. Although autobiographical, this poem does not tell us what 'really' happened – no autobiography can. All we can get is a version of events. Much stronger than the hints at crisis are the accusations Hardy makes about the suddenness of Emma's going, as though she should have told him in advance which would have made things somehow better. There is a strong sense in this poem (and even stronger in others in the sequence) that Hardy is re-telling the story to absolve himself of guilt. Suffering is one thing, guilty suffering another. And we must not forget that although the poem is about very private concerns, it was written for public consumption.

This sense of Hardy presenting a mythologised version of events leads neatly on to a **feminist** reading of the poem – as seen in the student response that the poem is 'essentially cynical, a public exercise in re-writing history, preparing the ground for the next relationship'. There are many aspects to feminist ideology, but essentially it challenges the traditional power of men and looks to celebrate the activities of women.

Knowing that Hardy was involved with another woman who was shortly to move in with him makes it harder to accept at face value his grief here. There is a strong sense of his blaming Emma here for not doing the accepted thing – of not giving him notice of her

161

intentions, of leading him to a spot which sickens him. This seems especially rich of him when we know that he went out of his way to avoid her in her bed-ridden state.

The fourth verse of *The Going* looks back to the time when Hardy first met Emma in Cornwall. Its focus on physical actions and appearance lacks intimacy. Emma is riding while he watches, and although she comes near and 'life unrolled us its very best' they do not speak. Indeed the poem is full of moments of not speaking: she did not speak 'that night'; they did not speak 'latterly'. The emphasis on outward appearance, of women as objects of desire, is seen in Emma being referred to as the 'swan-necked one'. Although this sounds approving, her illness made her neck particularly large; is Hardy really referring to her loss of beauty ?

A feminist reading of the poem would put the 'she' at the centre of discussion, seeing the poem as being about a woman whose identity is constructed purely through male values and attitudes. This idea of social construction comes close to the Marxist interpretation mentioned earlier.

Conclusion

Students who are used to having right answers may well be asking where this leaves us with *The Going*. Which approach is the right one to take? The 'right' answer to this question is 'none of them': all the approaches have something to offer, none of them definitively pins down the text for all readers for all time. You may well have an approach which particularly interests you, but if we are to subscribe to the idea that texts are full of potential meanings, then no single meaning can be defined. Instead we can juggle all the possible readings that have been identified in this chapter and realise that finding no single meaning makes the whole process of studying literature more open, more accessible, more collaborative – and more fun.

index of terms

The following technical terms have been used in this book. Using specific terminology when analysing texts can be very helpful, provided it is used accurately.

absence
This is used to refer to features of a text which you might expect to find, but are in fact not there.

ambiguity
The prefix 'ambi' literally means 'both'. Ambiguity with reference to textual analysis refers to the idea that texts can have more than one meaning, and that these meanings can co-exist together. Ambiguity in this sense is a positive term, rather than the negative way it is often used when having the sense of vagueness.

anthropomorphism
Sometimes called 'personification', this involves giving animals or objects feelings like those of a human being.

article
(definite and indefinite)
An article is any of three words which come before a noun – a, an, the. 'The' is the definite article, indicating a specific thing. 'A' and 'an' do not specify something specific, and so are indefinite articles.

chronological narrative
A chronological narrative tells a story in the time sequence in which events occurred.

connotation
Connotations are associations that are created by a word or phrase. Connotations can be individual but also cultural.

end-stopped	This refers to the end of a line of poetry coinciding with the end of a sentence or clause.
establishment	This refers to ways in which writers locate, at the beginning of texts, such things as characters, geographical settings, social settings and time.
graphology	This refers to the presentational features of texts, such as their shape, design, use of font etc.
ideology	A system of beliefs and ideas which is characteristic of a particular group or individual.
intertextuality	This refers to the ways in which one text echoes or carries references to other texts.
metaphor	The word 'metaphor' has a Greek origin, meaning transference. It applies a description to something where it is not literally applicable. It is based on the idea of similarity between things which are nonetheless different.
narrative structure	A narrative is a story, so narrative structure refers to the way the telling of the story is organised.
narrator/narratee	The narrator is the person in a text who appears to be addressing the reader (see 'persona' below). The narratee is the implied reader of a text, whose identity is built up by a series of assumptions that are made about the reader.
omniscient voice	This is a form of narrative in which the storyteller is not part of the action, but knows everything there is to know about it.
paradox	A paradox is a statement which appears to contradict itself, but in which both parts make sense.

persona
The persona is the invented voice which presents a narrative – the 'I' of a narrative which is not necessarily the voice of the author.

post-colonial
This refers to a way of looking at texts from a perspective which looks critically at the effects of colonisation.

pronoun reference
This involves the way cohesion works in a text. Once a specific reference has been made to a noun, a pronoun can then be used afterwards, i.e. 'Pope wrote the poem. He called it an epigram.' ('Pope' is followed by 'he' and 'poem' by 'it'.) Ambiguity can be created by making the reference unclear.

rhetorical question
A rhetorical question is a question which is asked, without the expectation of a reply.

rhyming couplet
When two consecutive lines of poetry rhyme, they are called rhyming couplets. This is especially the case if the whole poem consists of such rhyming parts, or if they are used to complete a poem or play.

syntax
The way sentences are constructed.